A Cicero Reader

LATIN Readers

Series Editor:
Ronnie Ancona, Hunter College and CUNY Graduate Center

These readers provide well annotated Latin selections written by experts in the field, to be used as authoritative introductions to Latin authors, genres, topics, or themes for intermediate or advanced college Latin study. Their relatively small size (covering approximately 600 lines) makes them ideal to use in combination. Each volume includes a comprehensive introduction, bibliography for further reading, Latin text with notes at the back, and complete vocabulary. There are nineteen volumes in the series. Check our website for updates: www.BOLCHAZY.com.

A Cicero Reader

Selections from Five Essays and Four Speeches, with Five Letters

James M. May

Bolchazy-Carducci Publishers, Inc.
Mundelein, Illinois USA

Series Editor: Ronnie Ancona

Volume Editor: Laurie Haight Keenan

Cover Design & Typography: Adam Phillip Velez

Maps: Mapping Specialists, Ltd.

A Cicero Reader
Selections from Five Essays and Four Speeches, with Five Letters

James M. May

Bolchazy-Carducci Publishers, Inc.
1570 Baskin Road
Mundelein, Illinois 60060
www.bolchazy.com

Printed in the United States of America
2016
by United Graphics

ISBN 978-0-86516-713-1

Library of Congress Cataloging-in-Publication Data

Cicero, Marcus Tullius.
A Cicero reader : selections from five essays and four speeches, with five letters / James M. May.
pages. cm. -- (Latin readers)
ISBN 978-0-86516-713-1 (pbk. : alk. paper) 1. Cicero, Marcus Tullius. I. May, James M. II. Cicero, Marcus Tullius. Works. Selections. Latin. 2012. III. Cicero, Marcus Tullius. Works. Selections. English. 2012. IV. Title. V. Series: Latin readers.
PA6307.A25M39 2012
875'.01--dc23

2012026878

Contents

List of Illustrations

Preface

The renowned, first-century teacher of rhetoric and oratory, Quintilian, tells us that a student should "realize that he has made substantial progress if he has become an avid admirer of Cicero" (*Institutio oratoria* 10.1.112). It is my hope that this slender text of selections from the writings of Cicero will aid students in making the kind of progress that Quintilian advocates. I must confess that, when the series editor, Professor Ronnie Ancona, approached me about authoring a Cicero Reader for this new series of Latin readers, I was more than a little skeptical. The amount of original Latin contained in the readers would be limited to about 600 lines of text. I wondered aloud to her how it would be possible for anyone to represent adequately the huge Ciceronian corpus, embracing so many, varied types of writing, in a mere 600 lines. And even if it were possible to select a number of passages wisely, effectively, and coherently, where would such a reader find an audience? Even in an intermediate reading class, 600 lines might be too few to fill an entire semester; while a more advanced class would consume the volume in a few weeks. Then there is the inherent problem that Cicero's works (except for selected letters) tend to be fairly lengthy—wouldn't most teachers, if possible, want to expose their students to a complete work of Cicero?

Professor Ancona did not flinch at these difficult questions. On the contrary, she explained to me the philosophy upon which the series was envisioned, and suggested some pedagogical situations in which such a text might be the perfect choice. I was intrigued by our discussion and agreed to think on it for a few days. As I contemplated it further, the possibilities became more and more exciting, and I became more and more enthusiastic about giving it a try. The volume that has resulted will, I hope, provide teachers and students with a number of options as they endeavor to improve Latin reading skills and learn more about Rome's greatest orator.

Passages have been selected from various works that characterize the Ciceronian corpus. The texts, for the most part, are not those that are most familiar to typical Latinists; yet, they endeavor to show Cicero in all his dimensions, some of which are perhaps less well known to the uninitiated—as orator, statesman, philosopher, man of letters, father and husband; and they aim at illustrating all registers of Ciceronian style. There is some special emphasis on a few of Cicero's favorite themes, viz., the value of liberal studies and the necessity of a comprehensive, universal education for the orator/statesman; the importance of the state and his identification with it; and the melancholy situation of the Republic in its waning years. For some time I debated about the arrangement of the passages; in the end, I opted for a chronological arrangement, rather than a thematic one, or one based on genre. This enables a more or less coherent picture of Cicero's life and career to emerge from beginning to end, a picture whose details can be supplemented through reading both the introductory paragraphs to each selection and the general introduction to Cicero's life and works.

I owe my sincere thanks to Ronnie Ancona for inviting me to be a part of this series, for her helpful guidance, and for her patience in dealing with a provost's unpredictable and oftentimes frustrating schedule; to Laurie Haight Keenen, the Bolchazy-Carducci production staff, and the press' anonymous readers for their valuable assistance, astute suggestions, and salutary corrections; to my students in our 2009 seminar on Cicero's prose, who piloted with me the first draft of these selections; to David Estle, who is chiefly responsible for compiling the Complete Vocabulary; and to my dear friend and colleague at St. Olaf College, Anne Groton, whose careful reading of the entire manuscript saved me from many errors and improved the final product significantly. I dedicate this volume to Ronald Karrenbauer and John Parks, Latin teachers extraordinaire, who first kindled in me a love for Cicero and Roman oratory and rhetoric.

James M. May
Northfield, Minnesota

Introduction

Cicero's life and works

Marcus Tullius Cicero, ancient Rome's greatest orator, was perhaps more successful and more abidingly influential as a practitioner of his art than any other speaker in any other age. The man whose name quickly became synonymous with eloquence itself (*non hominis nomen, sed eloquentiae,* see Quintilian, *Institutio oratoria* 10.1.112) left to his fellow Romans and to posterity a collection of speeches that serve as models of both effective courtroom persuasion and brilliantly lucid prose style. To categorize Cicero merely as an orator, however, would do a grave injustice to this consummate man of letters. As a theorist of oratory, he was not content to pass on precepts that would result in empty eloquence; Cicero required his ideal orator to be equipped with all the noble arts, demanding a union of eloquence and wisdom (i.e., rhetoric and philosophy). As a philosopher, although eclectic in approach and taste, and highly dependent on Greek models, Cicero presented his works from a distinctly Roman

Fig. 1. Bust of Marcus Tullius Cicero. Second century CE Roman copy of a late first century BCE original. Vatican Museum, Vatican State. Photo by James M. May.

point of view, and forged for the Latin language a philosophical vocabulary that would be utilized for centuries by subsequent writers. He likewise indulged in writing poetry and, despite the rather harsh judgment of posterity, was said (as reported by Plutarch, *Cicero* 2) to have been the finest poet of his day. And in the midst of this legal and literary activity, he maintained an incredibly active correspondence with his closest friend and confidant Atticus, his brother, and many other associates. His nearly one thousand extant letters are a veritable treasure-trove, providing us our greatest single source of information about Roman life and politics of that era. Although a *novus homo* ("new man") who had no ancestors who had attained high political office in Rome before him, Cicero remarkably managed to secure election to all the highest magistracies at the earliest eligible age. He remained on the stage of the Roman political scene of the late Republic, along with Pompey the Great, Crassus, Julius Caesar, Mark Antony, Octavian, and others, for most of his life. His dream of a harmony of social classes (*concordia ordinum*) and a consensus of like-minded patriots (*consensus omnium bonorum*), fashioned during his consulship and in subsequent years, was never ultimately realized. In the final analysis, like so many of his peers of the senatorial class, he was incapable of seeing beyond the social and political constructs of the nobility-dominated state, which he held so dear and of which he became almost a symbol: the death blow struck at Cicero's neck by the sword of Antony's henchman has, for many, appeared emblematic of the impending doom that awaited the Republic soon thereafter. As a man of letters as well as a man of action, Cicero inspired subsequent generations, not least of whom were the Renaissance humanists, who saw in his intellectual pursuits and loyal commitment to civic duty the traits that characterize one whom we still call a "Renaissance man."

Marcus Tullius Cicero was born on January 3, 106 BCE, at Arpinum, a town located about seventy miles southeast of Rome. His family, although technically not considered members of the Roman nobility, lived comfortably and had important connections (particularly through Cicero's mother, Helvia) in Rome. Cicero's father, a wealthy Roman knight (*eques*), was solicitous of his sons' education, and followed the typical Roman custom of entrusting their training, after the rudimentary instruction received in a Roman grammar school, to an influential and distinguished friend of the family. Marcus and his brother Quintus were received into the house of the famous orator and statesman, Lucius Crassus. There Cicero had the privilege of interacting not only with Crassus, but also Crassus' friends and associate, including most importantly Marcus Antonius, the other great orator of that generation, as well as L. Aelius Stilo, the famous Stoic teacher of grammar and rhetoric. In such circumstances, Cicero undoubtedly spent much of his youth in the Roman Forum, where he could witness and experience first-hand all aspects of Rome's forensic and political life.

After assuming the "toga of manhood" (*toga virilis*), Cicero served briefly in the military during the Social War (War with the Italian Allies). Returning after his service, he was formally introduced to Crassus' father-in-law, Q. Mucius Scaevola, "the Augur," who mentored him especially in the study of the civil law. In 88, he eagerly pursued the instruction of Philo of Larissa, head of the Academy at Athens, who had come to Rome. Philo's thought was skeptical in nature, holding that nothing could be entirely known for certain, and he advocated debating every issue from all sides. This approach exerted a profound influence on Cicero, an influence easily traceable in many of his subsequent writings. A few years later, Diodotus, the Stoic philosopher, took up residence in Cicero's house; from him he received training in various topics, especially in dialectic.

So, already as a teenager, Cicero had encountered an impressive array of thinkers—philosophers who were representative of the most important schools, as well as statesmen, orators, and rhetoricians, both Roman and Greek. He was practiced in speaking and writing both Greek and Latin, and had spent time composing and translating poetry. During this period, he also published his first work, *De inventione* (*On Invention*), a rhetorical treatise most likely completed by 88 BCE. The young man had initially intended to write the handbook on a grand scale, covering all parts of oratory, but he apparently lost interest in the project, and completed only two books. Nevertheless, *De inventione* is significant for the fact that it (along with the contemporary treatise known as the *Rhetorica ad Herennium*, which was mistakenly attributed to Cicero in the manuscript tradition) gives us a valuable view of first-century BCE rhetoric, as it was studied by Cicero and his peers. It is worth noting that, in the prologue to the work, Cicero already enunciates his strong belief in the importance of combining eloquence (i.e., rhetoric) with wisdom (i.e., philosophy), a conviction that will find its full expression in his mature rhetorical works. The treatise was extremely popular and exerted great influence during the Middle Ages.

Cicero most probably began pleading court cases at the age of twenty-four or twenty-five. His first extant oration dates from 81 BCE, and was delivered in a private case on behalf of a certain Quinctius (*Pro Quinctio*). In the following year, he entered the public arena with his first criminal case, defending Roscius of Ameria on a charge of parricide (*Pro Roscio Amerino*). In the politically charged atmosphere of the Sullan proscriptions and confiscations, Roscius (Cicero claims) was being framed by the actual murderers, who had killed his father and then placed his name on the proscription list, all in order to get their hands on his property. The mastermind behind the entire scheme was Chrysogonus, a freedman of the dictator Sulla. The more experienced and better known pleaders, according to Cicero, did not dare defend the backward, almost rustic Roscius in the face of Chrysogonus, a fact that again the young orator uses to his advantage, as he portrays himself as a courageous, outspoken defender of the downtrodden. Cicero's defense was successful and Roscius was acquitted.

It was for reasons of health and further study, not for fear of recrimination from Sulla stemming from the Roscius case (as Plutarch, *Cicero* 3, states), that Cicero set out for Greece and Asia Minor in 79 BCE, shortly after his early successes. He himself tells us (*Brutus* 313–314) that he was skinny and lacking in strength, with a long neck and weak lungs and voice, which he had strained by speaking continually without modulation and by holding his body tense throughout his entire delivery. Determined to gain strength and improve his speaking ability, he arrived in Athens and spent six months studying philosophy with Antiochus the Academic and rhetoric with Demetrius the Syrian. He then traveled through all of Asia Minor, where he practiced declamation with the most distinguished orators of the region. He moved on to Rhodes where he spent much time with Apollonius Molon, who effectively critiqued his speaking and worked to repress the youthful and sometimes excessively exuberant style evident in his early speeches. Cicero described the results in this way: "I returned after two years' absence not only better trained, but practically transformed. My voice was no longer excessively strained, my language had ceased to boil, my lungs had acquired strength, and my body had gained weight" (*Brutus* 316).

Back in Rome in 77 BCE, Cicero turned his attention once again to pleading court cases and preparing for a political career. His speech on behalf of the comic actor Roscius (*Pro Roscio comoedo*) dates from this period (*c.* 72 BCE), as well as the fragmentary oration for Tullius (*Pro Tullio*, probably delivered in 71 BCE). Now thirty years of age, Cicero was eligible to run for the quaestorship, the first magistracy in the succession of political offices (*cursus honorum*) that culminated in the consulship. He secured election and served as quaestor in western Sicily in 75 BCE, where he supervised the grain supply. His just and upright dealings in Sicily in combination with the connections he had made there during his service made him the Sicilians' choice as prosecutor when they initiated action against their former governor Verres on a charge of extortion.

Gaius Verres had been governor in Sicily in 73 BCE, but served two additional years because of the extraordinary political circumstances involved in the revolt of the slaves and gladiators led by Spartacus. During that time he was reputed to have extorted more than forty million sesterces, boasting that one year's proceeds were enough for him, and those gleaned from the second and third years were sufficient for his defenders and his judges. As a member of the senatorial class, he was supported by influential members of the Senate, and defended by Hortensius, Rome's premier orator at the time. Cicero generally preferred the role of advocate for the defense, but it was something of a practice in Rome for a rising politician to undertake the prosecution of a prominent figure in a noble cause. In this case, even while prosecuting, Cicero could again speak for the injured and cast himself in the role of the defender of the downtrodden. In preparing and carrying out the prosecution, Cicero displayed incredible energy. He first had to secure, through the process known as *divinatio*, the right to prosecute, which was challenged by one Q. Caecilius, Verres' former quaestor and certainly his preferred prosecutor for the case (preserved in the speech entitled *Divinatio in Q. Caecilium*). Next he had to gather evidence and build a case, all of which was resisted vigorously by Verres, Hortensius, and their supporters, who hoped to delay the case until Hortensius (who was a candidate for consul) and other powerful friends might gain even more influential positions in the government. Cicero himself was a candidate for the aedileship (which he won and served in 69 BCE), and so all of this had to be accomplished amid the pressures of running a campaign.

In the speech known as *In Verrem, Actio Prima* (*Against Verres, First Action*), delivered in 70 BCE, Cicero forgoes the usual heaping up of charges, vivid characterizations, and emotional appeal in favor of a lucid introduction to the case, its political and procedural difficulties, and a straightforward presentation of the evidence. Taken off guard by this approach, Hortensius failed in his repsonse, and Verres went into voluntary exile. The swift victory did not preclude Cicero from publishing five more speeches against Verres (*In Verrem, Actio Secunda*), cataloguing in great detail and with extraordinary rhetorical flourish the crimes and outrages of the governor. They are a rich storehouse, not only as oratorical models, but as an invaluable source for our knowledge of Roman provincial administration. The *Verrines* are an important turning point in Cicero's life and career. The decisive victory garnered for him considerable political support as well as the reputation of now being Rome's premier orator.

In 69 BCE, while serving his term as aedile, Cicero defended Aulus Caecina (*Pro Caecina*) in a complicated case involving ownership of property and the rights of heirs. Arguing the case required detailed knowledge of the civil law, of which Cicero was justly proud; he later cited this oration (*Orator* 102) as his own favorite example of a speech in the plain style. Cicero's defense of Marcus Fonteius (*Pro Fonteio*) on a charge of extortion in Gaul probably also occurred in this year.

The speech presents an interesting contrast with the *Verrines* in that Cicero employed several arguments on behalf of Fonteius that might well have been used in defending Verres.

Cicero's extant correspondence begins about this time and continues for nearly another twenty-five years, offering us a unique view of Roman politics and daily life. Once again a candidate for public office in 67 BCE, Cicero again was elected, ahead of all of his rivals, and served as praetor in 66. It was then that he delivered his first oration before the people (*De imperio Cn. Pompei, On Pompey's Command*, also known as *Pro lege Manilia, On the Manilian Law*), a speech supporting the proposal of the tribune Manilius to transfer the command of the war against King Mithridates of Pontus from Lucullus to Pompey the Great. Cicero seems to have been eager to display his allegiance to Pompey, an allegiance that would endure, in greater or lesser degree, throughout the rest of his life. The speech presents an idealized portrait of the general, praising his virtues of courage, authority, and good fortune (*virtus, auctoritas, felicitas*), while making every effort not to insult Lucullus and the senatorial party, the majority of whom opposed Manilius' law (which, in the end, was easily ratified). This year also was the occasion of Cicero's longest and perhaps most complicated defense-speech, delivered on behalf of Aulus Cluentius (*Pro Cluentio Habito*), charged with attempted poisoning of his stepfather, as well as earlier having bribed a jury to convict the same stepfather on a false charge of murder. The oration is a masterpiece of persuasion, filled with vivid narrations of familial relationships and feuds, detailed and lifelike portrayals of character, and skillful variations of style. The orator was particularly proud of his victory in this case, and later is reported to have boasted that he "had thrown dust in the eyes of the jury" (Quintilian, *Institutio oratoria* 2.17.21).

The decade of the 60s BCE was a particularly eventful time for Cicero. His son Marcus was born and his own father passed away; he was enjoying the hard-earned reputation of being Rome's premier orator; he had secured political prominence with his accession to the praetorship and his support of Pompey, the great general and leading figure among the conservative republican government. Now, as his year of eligibility grew closer, all of Cicero's attention turned to climbing to the top rung of the *cursus honorum*, the consulship. He worked hard and continuously to garner support from every possible corner. When the election results for the year 63 BCE were announced, and once again Marcus Tullius Cicero's name topped the list of those running for the consulship, Cicero had realized his dream. With the aid of his oratorical ability, hard work, and the support of the Roman knights (not to mention the threatening presence of Catiline on the same ballot, which shifted senatorial support to him), he had accomplished what only a handful of others in several previous generations had managed: a *novus homo*, the son of a Roman knight having no noble ancestors, secured at the youngest possible legal age Rome's highest political office. This accomplishment was one of the defining moments in Cicero's life. He was justly proud of it, and never ceased speaking about it—often to the dismay and irritation of his opponents and critics. It invested his character with a measure of prestige and authority that he would continuously wield in his subsequent oratorical and political career.

An extraordinary level of administrative and oratorical activity marked Cicero's consular year. In his first official act as consul, he opposed in three speeches an agrarian bill brought by the tribune Servilius Rullus (*De lege agraria contra Rullum*), which aimed, among other things, at dividing up the public land (*ager publicus*) in Campania. The first speech, which is fragmentary, is addressed to the Senate, the other two to the people in public meeting (*in contione*). Although Cicero repeatedly claims to be the true leader of popular sentiment (a *popularis*), advocating peace, harmony, and calm, while Rullus and the Board of Ten Commissioners are characterized as hypocrites who feign support of the people in order to further their own agenda, his pro-Pompey, senatorial sentiments are apparent. Cicero's strong support of senatorial policy was again displayed that year in his defense of Gaius Rabirius (*Pro Rabirio perduellionis reo*), an aged Roman knight and political scapegoat of sorts, who was charged with treason for having put to death Saturninus more than thirty-five years earlier (in 100 BCE). The motivation for the charge was to challenge the right of the Senate to act on the authority of its general decree of emergency (*senatus consultum ultimum*). Cicero valued his victory and his speech, which he cited as his finest example of the grand style (*Orator* 102). In a strange way, this challenge presaged the challenge that Cicero himself would subsequently face over the same issue involving the *senatus consultum ultimum* (SCU) only a few years later.

Towards the end of his year of office, Cicero, through careful attention, diligent investigation, and the fortunate confluence of a number of circumstances, uncovered a revolutionary plot to overthrow the government. Its leader was Lucius Sergius Catilina (who had been a rival of Cicero's in the consular elections), a disenchanted, bankrupt senator of noble descent, who, despite Cicero's characterization of him, possessed considerable intellectual and physical abilities and a personal magnetism that was capable of attracting a loyal following. The four speeches that the consul delivered concerning the conspiracy, known as the *Catilinarian Orations* (*In Catilinam I–IV*), are justly famous and familiar to most every student who has studied Latin. The first, delivered to the Senate on November 8 following an abortive attempt to assassinate Cicero in his home, is a frontal attack aimed at Catiline, who came—probably unexpectedly—to the Senate meeting on that day. Cicero, seeing Catiline seated in isolation from the rest of the senators, began his speech with an unorthodox series of rhetorical questions, *Quousque tandem abutere, Catilina, patientia nostra*? ("How long, Catiline, will you continue to abuse our patience?"), and proceeded to inform the Senate of the conspiracy, while urging Catiline to go into voluntary exile. The second speech, delivered to the people on the next day, informed them of the plot and the actions taken by Cicero to insure their safety, while presenting vivid portraits of the savage conspirators and the ever-provident consul. The third speech, given to the people on December 3, was precipitated by the arrest of several conspirators along with the apprehension of crucially incriminating evidence. Two days later, on the Nones of December, the Senate met to debate the fate of the conspirators. Caesar, among others, argued against execution, while Cicero, armed with the *senatus consultum*, argued strenuously in the *Fourth Catilinarian* in favor of it; it was, however, the speech of Cato the Younger that carried the day, and that evening the five conspirators in custody, including a praetor, Cornelius Lentulus Sura, were strangled to death in the Tullianum, Rome's prison. Cicero is said, upon emerging from the scene, to have delivered his shortest speech: *Vixerunt* ("They have lived").

It is rather amazing that, amid the flurry of activity during the conspiracy, sometime between the delivery of the *Second* and *Third Catilinarian*, Cicero was called upon to defend the consul-elect for 62 BCE, Lucius Murena, on a charge of bribery. The rhetorical challenges facing Cicero were daunting: the case could not have come at a more inconvenient time; the charges were being leveled by two of Cicero's own friends and supporters, Servius Sulpicius (whom Cicero, in fact, had supported for election against Murena!) and Marcus Cato the Younger; and finally, the realization that if Murena was convicted, the new year would begin with only one consul in office, while the state was still embroiled in the conspiracy. The speech that resulted (*Pro Murena*) is one of Cicero's rhetorical masterpieces, wherein he neutralizes the powerful authority of the prosecutors with the genial wit for which he was famous, poking fun at Sulpicius as a professional lawyer and Cato as an overly rigid Stoic, all the while maintaining the crucial plea that the new year must open with two consuls at the helm of state. Cicero's victory was overwhelming, and Murena served as consul in 62.

Following the execution of the conspirators, a public thanksgiving was decreed and Cicero was hailed as *Pater Patriae* ("Father of the Fatherland"). Yet only a few weeks later, when laying down his office on December 31, he was prevented by the tribune Q. Metellus Nepos from addressing the people in customary fashion, on the grounds that, by executing the conspirators, he had put to death Roman citizens without a trial. Making the best of the situation, Cicero confined himself to the oath that he had performed the duties of the consulship faithfully, swearing that by his efforts the city and the state had been saved. The people roared their approval, but storm clouds lingered on the horizon. A year later, Publius Clodius Pulcher, a patrician descended from one of the noblest families of Rome, was caught disgracefully dressed as a woman at the rites in honor of the Bona Dea, from which men were strictly barred. In the subsequent judicial investigation, Clodius, on trial for sacrilege, claimed to have been ninety miles away from Rome at the time. Cicero, however, had seen him in Rome within three hours of the time of his alibi, and testified to that effect. Despite this testimony and the obvious guilt of Clodius, a bribed jury acquitted the perpetrator. Exacerbating the enmity between them, Cicero, employing his characteristic quick repartee and caustic wit, humiliated Clodius publicly in the Senate on a subsequent occasion. Clodius, however, would soon have his revenge.

At about this same time, the Senate obstinately (and shortsightedly) had snubbed the requests of three of its most powerful members, Pompey, Caesar, and Crassus; these actions led to the formation (in 60 BCE) of the coalition among these men known to history as the "First Triumvirate." Cicero himself was courted by Caesar as a fourth member of the group, certainly on the strength of his legal knowledge and powers of persuasion, but the orator could not bring himself to support in an active way Caesar's manipulation of the constitution. In fact, he spoke out against it. Then in 59 BCE, Clodius (a noble patrician by birth) arranged to have himself adopted into a plebeian family in order to allow him to run for the office of tribune (which was open only to plebeians). Cicero may have seen the handwriting on the wall, but he refused to acknowledge it. As late as November of 59, he expressed confidence in his future. He even refused a generous offer from Caesar to become one of his deputies (*legatus*) in Gaul or a commissioner for supervising the division of public lands. Clodius secured the office of tribune and the support of the consuls for 58 BCE, L. Piso and A. Gabinius, in order to avenge himself. Finally, in March of 58, Clodius arranged for passage of a law that outlawed from Rome anyone who had put Roman citizens to death without a trial. The Senate was powerless, and help from the consuls and triumvirs (who were content to have Cicero removed from the scene for a time) was not forthcoming. Cicero decided to leave Rome, retiring into exile in northern Greece. A second law, naming Cicero specifically (and hence unconstitutional) was passed shortly thereafter. Clodius then engineered the razing of Cicero's house on the Palatine, managing to have part of the property consecrated as a shrine to Liberty. Other properties owned by him suffered damage as well, and his wife and children were forced to take shelter with relatives.

Only three speeches survive to us from the years between Cicero's consulship and his exile. In 62 BCE, Cicero defended Publius Sulla (*Pro Sulla*) on a charge of complicity in the Catilinarian conspiracy. The speech illustrates important tactics that will become staples of Ciceronian persuasive strategy, namely the increased use of Cicero's own character (ethos), now enhanced by consular prestige, as a source for proof, as well as Cicero's identification with his client in order to lend more authority to the character and case of his client. Cicero's defense of Sulla depends a great deal on the argument that he himself, the enemy of the conspiracy, is speaking on behalf of Sulla; Sulla must therefore be innocent. One of the orator's most beloved speeches, his defense of Archias the poet (*Pro Archia poeta*), also dates from 62. Cicero is technically defending Archias' claim to citizenship, but the speech in large part is a stirring and eloquent defense of the study of literature and the liberal arts. The *Pro Flacco*, delivered in 59 BCE, is Cicero's defense of a friend (who had assisted in the apprehension of the Catilinarian conspirators) and former governor of the province of Asia on a charge of extortion. Cicero employs humor in combination with a kindling of Roman prejudice against the provincials and an effective use of consular authority to secure the acquittal of a client who was probably guilty.

It was psychologically devastating for Cicero to deal with the fact that his crushing of the Catilinarian conspiracy, the crowning glory of his consulship, was, likewise, the cause of his forced departure from Rome. The year and a half that he spent in exile was the low point of his life. Letters from that period to his friend and confidant Atticus reveal an unseemly, yet understandable mood of depression that led him even to contemplate suicide. Friends and supporters in Rome, however, were not lacking. The consuls and tribunes of 57 BCE were favorable to Cicero's cause, and Pompey, who had done nothing to throttle Clodius' previous attacks, was now irritated by his actions and actively supported the recall. On August 4, 57 BCE, the law was passed authorizing his return; a month later, Cicero arrived in Rome amid an atmosphere of great triumph. He immediately set about reestablishing his private and public standing.

The speeches delivered during this time are generally known collectively as *post reditum*. He formally thanked the Senate on the day after his return (*Post reditum in senatu*); on the next day, he addressed the people from the rostra, and expressed his thanks to them (*Post reditum ad quirites*). *De domo sua* (*On His House*) was delivered before the college of priests and argued for the recovery of Cicero's property on the Palatine and the illegality of its consecration to Liberty at the instigation of Clodius. *De haruspicum responso* (*On the Reply of the Soothsayers*) was delivered in the Senate in 56 BCE, and responded to Clodius' assertion that Cicero had offended the gods by restoring his house on a consecrated site. These speeches, as well as the others dating from this period, are marked by certain themes that resonate continually throughout them. They are often characterized by being as much apologies on behalf of Cicero as political deliberations or defenses of clients. Cicero presents himself as the consular orator who now has saved the state twice without recourse to arms, once through his thwarting of Catiline, the second time by his voluntary departure from Rome (to keep the peace, as he claims). At times he identifies himself closely with the state; at other times, he presents himself as the sacrificial victim who was offered up on its behalf.

The fine speech delivered (March 56 BCE) in defense of Publius Sestius (*Pro Sestio*), the former tribune who had championed the cause for Cicero's recall, and who had been indicted for violence, illustrates all of these points. In addition to offering a defense of Sestius and an *apologia* on his own behalf, Cicero sets forth a stunning manifesto of his political philosophy, wherein, among other things, he effectively characterizes the *optimates*, or "best men" (who support the senatorial and constitutional government of the Republic), as well as the band of thugs and revolutionaries, supporters of men like Clodius, who call themselves *populares* ("friends of the people"). The speech was followed by the *In Vatinium* (*Against Vatinius*), a scathing, invective-filled cross-examination of the former tribune and supporter of Caesar who had testified against Sestius. A month later, Cicero was at his oratorical best in his justly famous defense of Marcus Caelius, a young protégé who had been charged with several counts of violence (*Pro Caelio*). Leaving behind the politics of exile and restoration, Cicero presented a successful defense based largely on clever characterizations of Caelius, Clodia (according to Cicero, the real force behind the prosecution), and even Clodius (her brother), along with their noble ancestors.

Elated by his successful recall, the recovery of his building site and damages for the loss of his house and estates, and the recent overwhelming victory in the Sestius case, and further encouraged by what he perceived as a growing rift among the triumvirs, Cicero proposed, the day after his speech for Caelius, that the Senate should re-open the discussion of Caesar's distribution of the Campanian land. Once again Cicero had miscalculated the strength of the optimate position and their ability to foil the will of the triumvirs. His action precipitated the so-called conference of Luca, a meeting held in order to patch up their differences. Cicero was soon brought to heel following an encounter between Pompey and Cicero's brother Quintus. Pompey called in all his markers, so to speak, reminding Quintus of the pledges he had given (about Marcus' future conduct) when he had lobbied for his brother's recall; Pompey made it clear that Marcus' silence, if not his cooperation, was expected. As a result, Cicero, crestfallen and humiliated, withdrew his motion and, for the next several years, presented no opposition to the three. In fact, he was forced into delivering (in June or July of 56 BCE) what he called his "palinode" or "recantation" (see *Ad Att.* 4.5), perhaps the speech *De provinciis consularibus* (*On the Consular Provinces*), in which he argued for an extension of Caesar's Gallic command. He was all too aware of the inconsistency of his actions, and he found it embarrassingly exasperating, as he candidly revealed in private conversations and letters.

Later, he was again called upon to defend partisans of the triumvirs, Balbus (in the *Pro Balbo*), Vatinius (whom he had attacked so fiercely only two years previously), Aulus Gabinius (the consular colleague of Piso who in 58 BCE had aided and abetted Clodius' measures against him), and Rabirius (in the *Pro Rabirio Postumo*). Two other orations dating from this period are worthy of mention: The *Pro Scauro* (54 BCE), given in defense of Scaurus on a charge of extortion, again stirs up prejudices against the provincials, this time the Sardinians, in an emotionally charged proceeding. The *Pro Plancio* (54 BCE) is Cicero's defense of the man who, four years earlier as quaestor in Macedonia, had given Cicero aid during the dark hours of his exile. As is the case in so many of Cicero's speeches, the actual charge of election bribery retreats into the background, giving way to the presentation of Cicero's own character, his deeds, and the authority with which he supports his client.

How does one deal with such trying times of personal inconsistency, not to mention the humiliating realization of having gravely compromised one's principles? For Cicero, his consolation was always the same: he took refuge in literature, returning to his youthful studies of rhetoric and philosophy, and writing about them. During the half-decade following Luca, he composed three important treatises, *De oratore* (*On the Ideal Orator*), *De republica* (*On the Republic*), and *De legibus* (*On the Laws*). The three books that comprise *De oratore*, Cicero's finest and most important rhetorical treatise, were begun in 55 BCE and completed the following year. The dramatic date of the dialogue is 91 BCE, and Cicero set the discussion at the Tusculan estate of his former mentor, the legendary orator Crassus, who is joined by Antonius, the other great orator of the age, Scaevola "the Augur," and several other prominent speakers and men of state. The treatise is unique among ancient rhetorical writings in that it abandons entirely the format and the language—that is, the jargon—of typical rhetorical handbooks. In fact, Cicero has his characters openly criticize the handbooks virtually every opportunity they get. Still, most of the rhetorical precepts (at least in abbreviated form) are there, woven skillfully into the dialogue and discussed in a vocabulary that avoids the traditional technical terminology. In the course of the discussion, a portrait of the ideal orator emerges, a man in possession of both eloquence and wisdom, steeped not only in the knowledge of rhetoric, but more importantly one who has studied philosophy, law, human character and emotion, in short, all of the noble arts, the product of a cultural education that has prepared him to speak on any topic and assume any position of leadership in the state. In many ways, of course, this portrait is made in Cicero's own image and likeness, and it, along with the work as a whole, stands as a monument to his rhetorical and oratorical genius.

By 54 BCE, Cicero was already engaged in another dramatic dialogue, the *De republica,* this time set in 129 BCE, with Scipio the Younger and others of his friends serving as interlocutors. Originally disposed in six books, parts of the work are unfortunately lost. Book 1 outlines the three forms of constitutions, democracy, aristocracy, and monarchy, and judges the Roman Republic, a composite of the three, as the finest constitutional form. Rome's course in developing such a constitution is traced in Book 2; Book 3 contains an argument over whether justice depends on expediency, while Book 4, largely fragmentary, deals with education and culture within the community. The final two books, also fragmented, present the picture of the ideal statesman and his rewards, culminating with the justly celebrated "Dream of Scipio" (*Somnium Scipionis*), in which Scipio relates how his adoptive grandfather, the great Africanus, appeared to him in a dream and revealed to him a view of the universe, the immortality of the soul, and a promise of an eternal reward amid the harmony of the spheres for those who have served the community and their fellows well. The *De legibus,* begun probably in 53 or 52 BCE but interrupted by Cicero's subsequent governorship and the Civil War, is something of a sequel to the *De republica.* Inspired by Plato's *Laws,* this dialogue between Cicero, his brother, and Atticus explores the general nature of law and justice, religious law, and laws affecting magistrates. Only three books survive of the original five or six. In addition to his writings, Cicero's only other consolation during this time was his election as augur in 53 BCE.

While Cicero was writing about the ideal state and its laws, the Roman state, during the same time, was in chaos, embroiled in bribery, political maneuverings, disorder, and violence. Elections had been repeatedly postponed because of the unrest, and riots between rival gangs, headed by Clodius and Milo, a candidate for office and friend of Cicero (who had, as tribune, worked for his recall from exile), were frequent. In January 52 BCE, the companies of Clodius and Milo met, probably by accident, on the Appian Way; fighting broke out, and in the scuffle, Clodius was killed. To control the further unrest that ensued, Pompey was appointed sole consul and enforced strict measures to govern the subsequent judicial proceedings. Cicero delivered his speech on Milo's behalf (*Pro Milone*) in a packed forum under the eye of Pompey and his armed guard. Visibly shaken by the circumstances, he completed his speech, but not with his accustomed effectiveness. Milo was convicted and went into exile. The speech as transmitted to us is an extraordinary rhetorical composition, employing the three modes of persuasion—logical argumentation, portrayal of character (ethos), and appeal to the emotions (pathos)—to near perfection.

Unlike many Roman magistrates, Cicero never had a desire to leave Rome as a governor of a province. He had refused such duty after his praetorship and consulship. But in March of 51 BCE, much to his dismay, he was sent as proconsul to the large province of Cilicia in Asia Minor. Upon his arrival, he found matters, both civil and military, in much disarray. He set about restoring order, fixing reasonable interest rates, and fighting extortion. Faced with the threat of a possible invasion by the Parthians, he shored up his military forces and undertook a small campaign against the hill-tribes of Mt. Amanus. After a siege of fifty-seven days, he captured the stronghold and was granted a *supplicatio* (a public thanksgiving) by the Senate. Although he long cherished hopes for a triumph, these were never realized.

Cicero returned to Rome in early January of 49 BCE to find the political situation in turmoil and the state on the brink of civil war. Crassus had been killed in Parthia in 53 BCE, and the relationship between Pompey and Caesar, so often strained in the past, had now reached the breaking point. Even after Caesar had crossed the Rubicon, Cicero hoped to be able to negotiate some sort of reconciliation that might secure peace. Appointed by the government as district commissioner at Capua, he spent the next several weeks away from the city, in Campania and at his estate in Formiae, debating with himself, in true Academic fashion, his best course of action. He realized that war, no matter the victor, would precipitate confiscation, bloodshed, and proscription; he could not stomach the unconstitutionality of Caesar's actions, but was equally repulsed by many of the deeds of Pompey's supporters. On March 28, Caesar himself visited Cicero at Formiae and requested that he come to Rome to work for peace. The orator frankly set forth conditions that Caesar could not accept, and in the end, Cicero did not go to Rome; eventually he joined the republican forces in Greece. After Caesar's victory at Pharsalus on August 9, 48 BCE (from which Cicero was absent because of illness), and having subsequently refused command of the army proposed to him by Cato, Cicero returned to Italy, passing a year fraught with anxiety in Brundisium. In September of 47, Caesar returned and graciously gave Cicero permission to remain in the country.

Cicero abstained from politics under the dictatorship of Caesar. In 46 BCE, however, he broke a six-year period of silence by delivering in the Senate the *Pro Marcello* (*For Marcellus*), which is actually not a defense of Marcellus (who had been an opponent of Caesar), but a panegyric in praise of Caesar's clemency. This is the first of the so-called "Caesarian Speeches." The other two, the *Pro Ligario* (a beautifully crafted, cleverly argued speech defending Ligarius for waging war in Africa against Caesar), and the *Pro rege Deiotaro* of 45 BCE (defending King Deiotarus, who was charged with the attempted murder of Caesar some years before), are forensic speeches both delivered before Caesar, who as dictator had assumed extraordinary judicial authority.

The troubles that Cicero faced in his public, political life during this period were compounded seriously by the troubles he experienced in his own private life. After thirty years of marriage, he divorced his wife Terentia in 46 BCE, the culmination of an estrangement that had begun several years before. He almost immediately married the young Publilia, but then came the greatest blow, the loss of Tullia, his beloved daughter, who died from complications of childbirth. Cicero's grief at the death of his daughter was nearly inconsolable, and Publilia's lack of sympathetic support led quickly to divorce. Once again, as he had done a decade earlier, he took refuge in philosophy and literature. Writing day and night because he could not sleep, Cicero's literary output during the next two years was absolutely astounding. Among lost works, the *Consolatio,* a record of the deaths of great figures, inspired by the death of Tullia, and the *Hortensius,* a protreptic to the study of philosophy that would later have a profound impact on St. Augustine, are most noteworthy.

In rhetoric, he composed two works that can rightly take their place alongside *De oratore. Brutus* (46 BCE) presents an invaluable history of Roman oratory that is detailed by Cicero's critical assessment of orators of the past, along with a few of his own day; *Orator* (46 BCE), again dedicated to M. Brutus, presents a portrait of the perfect orator. We find in both these works essentially a corroboration of oratorical principles as set forth ten years earlier in *De oratore,* but the emphasis here has shifted to questions of style. During the intervening decade, a classicizing movement known as Atticism (or neo-Atticism) had gained prominence; it recommended (largely in reaction to oratory like Cicero's) employing a simpler style of speaking and models (especially the Attic orator Lysias) that fostered such a style. In these works, Cicero answers such critics, claiming that the neo-Atticists have abandoned practical persuasion for stylistic nicety. According to Cicero, the consummate Attic orator was Demosthenes, the master of all three styles (plain, middle, and grand), and it is his kind of oratory that must be emulated. Another minor work, *De optimo genere oratorum*, an introduction to a proposed (but apparently never completed) translation of Aeschines' *Against Ctesiphon* and Demosthenes' *On the Crown*, also dates from this period.

Still even more impressive is the range, scope, and number of philosophical treatises composed during this time. The *Paradoxa Stoicorum* of 46 BCE is a brief treatment of six paradoxes of Stoic philosophy (e.g., the wise man alone is rich), exploring Stoic doctrine, which had always been of interest to him. *De finibus bonorum et malorum* (*On the Supreme Good*, 45 BCE) examines in five books the question of the highest good. L. Manlius Torquatus expounds the Epicurean doctrine in Book 1, which is refuted by Cicero in Book 2. M. Porcius Cato explains Stoic doctrine in Book 3, which in turn is refuted again by Cicero in Book 4, while M. Pupius Piso explains the Academic and Peripatetic views in Book 5. Such mode of argumentation and presentation was a standard of operation for student of the Academy, which, skeptical of one's ability to discover absolute truth, advocated arguing every point from every possible angle in order to arrive at a view that was closest to the truth. Of all philosophical approaches, this was the most compatible to Cicero's nature and his preferred method of dealing with most questions, in his treatises and even in making his own private decisions. The *Tusculan Disputations* (45 BCE), named for Cicero's estate where the discussions are set, consider in five books the nature of death, the endurance of pain, how wisdom fortifies a person from sorrow and mental anguish, and why virtue is sufficient to secure happiness. The *Academica* (45 BCE) has come down to us as a conflation of two editions, changing the interlocutors from Catulus, Lucullus, and Hortensius in the first edition to Varro and Cicero himself in the second. The work explores the epistemology of skepticism and the Old, Middle, and New Academies. *De natura deorum* (*On the Nature of the Gods,* 45 BCE) is a dialogue set in 77 BCE, which examines the theological views of the Epicurean, Stoic, and Academic schools. Again the interlocutors (here Velleius the Epicurean, Balbus the Stoic, and Cotta the Academic) present their own views of the subject, which are then debated, discussed, or refuted by one of their peers. Its chief importance lies in the fact that it presents to us the religious thought of an educated Roman of the late Republic.

Cicero was not present on the Ides of March, 44 BCE, when Caesar was assassinated, but he certainly rejoiced in the deed: "How I wish you had invited me to that splendid banquet on the Ides of March!," he would later write Trebonius (*Ad fam.* 10.28). On March 17, Cicero delivered a speech in the Senate urging a general amnesty for the conspirators, like that declared in Athens after the expulsion of the Thirty Tyrants. The arrival in Rome of the young C. Octavius, Caesar's adopted son and heir, further buoyed the hopes of those supporting the Republic. But Marcus Antonius (Mark Antony), who had been Caesar's colleague in the consulship and had, after the assassination, gained possession of Caesar's political papers and private fortune, continued to strengthen his own position. Cicero soon found himself losing hope, in fear that Rome had merely substituted one tyrant for another. Again he turned to philosophy. He completed the *De divinatione* (*On Divination*), which he had begun before the Ides of March, presenting arguments in favor of the Roman practice of augury in the first book (in the character of his brother Quintus), and against divination (in his own character) in the second book. The fragmentary *De fato* (*On Fate*), whose most interesting aspect is Cicero's spirited defense of free will, also dates from this time, as do two other short treatises that are recognized universally as Cicero's most charming efforts, the *De senectute* (*On Old Age*) and the *De amicitia* (*On Friendship*), both of which are dedicated to Atticus. Cicero set his discussion of old age in 150 BCE, at the house of the famous statesman Cato the Elder, who, speaking with Laelius and Scipio, goes on to refute the reasons why people generally consider old age to be an unhappy time. In *De amicitia,* Laelius, at his home in 129 BCE, discusses the topic of friendship with Fannius and Scaevola "the Augur." Both of these works have been extremely popular throughout the ages, and have served perennially as school texts, a fact that is easily understood considering the elegance of their prose, their convenient length, and their enduringly relevant subject matter.

It was also during this time (44 BCE) that Cicero began his last, and perhaps most influential philosophical treatise, the *De officiis* (*On Moral Duties*), written not in dialogue form, but as an expository epistle to his son. The first book discusses the cardinal virtues of wisdom, justice, fortitude, and temperance. According to Cicero, the human race is a community bound together by the ties of speech and reason. Humans should employ speech and reason (or eloquence and wisdom) for the advancement of their community, which is more important than any one individual. Book 2 speaks of duties, and discusses the notion of *utile,* the expedient, which cannot be divorced from the honorable (*honestum*). Book 3 explores the question of the apparent conflict between the expedient and the honorable, in which Cicero maintains that such conflict is only an imagined one, seeing that what is dishonorable or wrong can never really be expedient. The *De officiis* is perhaps one of Cicero's most original, and in many ways most "Roman" of philosophical treatises, setting forth for his son a kind of blueprint for the man of action in private and public life. It exerted a tremendous influence on Western humanistic culture.

Many thoughts about duties, the honorable and the expedient must have been swirling about in Cicero's mind, when in July of 44 BCE, on his way to Greece, and hearing news that a reconciliation between Antony and the conspirators was probable, he decided to turn back in order to attend the senate meeting scheduled for September 1. (It was, incidentally, during one leg of this truncated trip to Greece, the sea voyage from Velia to Rhegium, that Cicero wrote, from memory and without the aid of books, his *Topica*, dedicated to Trebatius, an Aristotelian inspired treatise that presents topics for oratorical arguments, e.g., more and less, time past, present, and future, contraries, likenesses, etc.). Back in Rome, he found the situation less promising than he had hoped, and decided not to attend the meeting, claiming that he was ill. Antony, angry at his absence, delivered a speech against him, and made offerings to the deified Caesar. On the next day, September 2, 44 BCE, Cicero took the first step on a journey from which there would be no turning back when he answered Antony (who was absent) with the *First Philippic,* a speech critical of Antony, though free of harsh personal attack. Cicero's final sentence proved an appropriate valediction for the final year of his life: "For myself, what life I have lived is pretty much enough, whether in years or in glory. If more is to come, it will come not so much for me as for you and the Republic."

Antony retired to prepare his reply, which he delivered in the Senate on September 19, 44. Cicero countered with his celebrated *Second Philippic*, a scathing invective showing no restraint, which he sent to Atticus for approval in late October. The speech was never delivered, but published as a pamphlet in late November. It is worth noting that Cicero himself referred to his speeches against Antony as "Philippics" (*Ad Brut.* 2.4), purposely drawing a comparison between these attacks on Antony and those that the great Greek orator Demosthenes had made on Philip II of Macedon, three hundred years earlier. From this point on, all of Cicero's energies were directed to rousing the senatorial order in hopes of recapturing the spirit and the glory of the languishing Republic. During the next half year, Cicero delivered twelve more *Philippics*, two to the people and ten to the Senate, all aimed in one way or another at warding off any sort of reconciliation between the Senate and Antony. These orations are marked by great clarity of style and purposefulness, and they rely heavily on presentation of character and emotion for their effectiveness. The ethos of Cicero the patriot is there again, marked now by a reinvigorated sincerity and intensity of purpose; Antony, like Cicero's previous adversaries (Verres, Catiline, Clodius, et al.), represents all things un-Roman, even inhuman, and personifies the forces of despotism, madness, evil, and darkness.

That this type of eloquence had the power to move hearts is readily confirmed by subsequent events. In the end, of course, Cicero's hopes were dashed, yet the effect of his oratory lingered, enough so that its target felt the need to exact vengeance. After the trio of Antony, Lepidus, and Octavius had sealed their compact and were appointed commissioners for the reorganization of the state in November (a compact known as the Second Triumvirate), they immediately set about removing their enemies from the scene. Cicero's name appeared prominently on the list of proscribed (despite, according to Plutarch, the objections of Octavian). At first, Cicero thought of fleeing to the East, but after a half-hearted attempt to escape, he ordered his slaves to stand aside, and with these words, "Let me die in the country that I have so often saved" (Livy 120.50), he offered his neck to Antony's minions (December 7, 43 BCE). His head and hands were carried back to Rome, and, to the horror of the people, nailed to the Rostra, where Antony's wife further disfigured them.

Perhaps Caesar Augustus, formerly known as Octavian, an ultimate if not entirely willing collaborator in the destruction of Cicero and the Republic, provided the most succinct and fitting valediction for the great orator. Many years after Cicero's death, the emperor spied his grandson trying to hide a scroll of one of Cicero's works under the folds of his toga. "Seeing it, he took it from the boy and read through a great part as he stood there; then giving it back to the lad, he said, 'This was an eloquent man, my child, an eloquent man and a lover of his country'" (Plutarch, *Cicero* 49).

Suggested reading

Alexander, M. C. *Trials in the Late Roman Republic, 149 BC to 50 BC.* Toronto, Buffalo, London, 1990.

Axer, J. "Tribunal-Stage-Arena: Modeling of the Communications Situation in M. Tullius Cicero's Judicial Speeches." *Rhetorica* 7 (1989): 299–311.

Bailey, D. R. Shackleton. *Cicero.* New York: Scribner, 1971.

———, ed. *Cicero, Epistulae ad Familiares.* 2 vols. Cambridge, 1977.

———, ed. *Cicero: Epistulae ad Quintum Fratrem et M. Brutum.* Cambridge, London, New York, New Rochelle, Melbourne, Sydney, 1980.

Classen, J. –M. "Cicero's Banishment: Tempora et Mores." *Acta Classica: Proceedings of the Classical Association of South Africa* 35 (1992): 19–47.

Clark, M. E., and J. S. Ruebel. "Philosophy and Rhetoric in Cicero's *Pro Milone.*" *Rheinisches Museum für Philologie* 128 (1985): 57–72.

Connolly, Joy. *The State of Speech: Rhetoric and Political Thought in Ancient Rome.* Princeton and Oxford, 2007.

Corbeill, A. *Controlling Laughter: Political Humor in the Late Roman Republic.* Princeton, 1996.

Craig, C. P. *Form as Argument in Cicero's Speeches: A Study of Dilemma.* Atlanta, 1993.

———. "Shifting Charge and Shifty Argument in Cicero's Speech for Sestius." In *The Orator in Action and Theory in Greece and Rome (Studies in Honor of George A Kennedy)*, edited by C. W. Wooten, 111–22. Mnemosyne Supplement, 225. Leiden, 2001.

———. "A Survey of Selected Recent Work on Cicero's Rhetorica and Speeches." In *Brill's Companion to Cicero: Oratory and Rhetoric,* edited by J. M. May, 503–31; followed by a comprehensive bibliography of Ciceronian oratory and rhetoric, 533–599. Leiden, 2002.

Crawford, J. W. *M. Tullius Cicero: The Lost and Unpublished Orations.* Göttingen, 1984.

Crook, J. A., A. Lintott, and E. Rawson, eds. *The Cambridge Ancient History, Vol. IX, The Last Age of the Roman Republic, 146–43 B.C.* 2nd ed. Cambridge, MA, 1994.

Dominik, W., and J. Hall, eds. *A Companion to Roman Rhetoric.* Oxford, 2007.

Dorey, T. A., ed. *Cicero.* Studies in Latin Literature and Its Influence. London, 1964.

Dugan, J. "How to Make (and Break) a Cicero: *Epideixis*, Textuality, and Self-fashioning in the *Pro Archia* and *In Pisonem.*" *Classical Antiquity* 20 (2001): 35–77.

———. *Making a New Man: Ciceronian Self-Fashioning in the Rhetorical Works.* Oxford, 2005.

Dyck, A. R. *A Commentary on Cicero,* De Officiis. Ann Arbor, 1996.

———. "Narrative, Obfuscation, Philosophical *Topoi*, and Tragic Patterning in Cicero's *Pro Milone.*" *Harvard Studies in Classical Philology* 98 (1998): 219–41.

Fantham, E. *The Roman World of Cicero's* De Oratore. Oxford, 2004.

Gotoff, H. C. *Cicero's Elegant Style: An Analysis of the* Pro Archia. Urbana, 1979.

Gruen, E. *The Last Generation of the Roman Republic.* Berkeley, 1974.

Habicht, C. *Cicero the Politician.* Baltimore and London, 1990.

Hall, J. *Politeness and Politics in Cicero's Letters.* Oxford, 2009.

Hutchinson, G. O. *Cicero's Correspondence: A Literary Study.* Oxford, 1998.

Kaster, R. A. *Cicero: Speech on Behalf of Publius Sestius.* New York, Oxford, 2006.

Kennedy, G. A. "The Rhetoric of Advocacy in Greece and Rome." *American Journal of Philology* 89 (1968): 419–36.

———. *The Art of Rhetoric in the Roman World.* Princeton, 1972.

Konstan, D. "Rhetoric and the Crisis of Legitimacy in Cicero's Catilinarian Orations." In *Rethinking the History of Rhetoric: Multidisciplinary Essays on the Rhetorical Tradition*, edited by T. Poulakos, 11–30. Boulder, San Francisco, Oxford, 1993.

Leach, E. W. "The Spectacula of Cicero's *Pro Sestio*: Patronage, Production and Performance." In *Rome and Her Monuments: Essays on the City and Literature of Rome in Honor of Katherine A. Geffcken*, edited by S. K. Dickison and J. P. Hallett, 369–97. Wauconda, IL, 2000.

Leeman, A. D. "The Structure of Cicero's *De Oratore I*." In *Ciceroniana. Hommages à Kazimierz Kumaniecki*, edited by A. Michel and R. Verdière, 140–49. Leiden, 1975.

Lintott, A. W. "Cicero and Milo." *Journal of Roman Studies* 64 (1974): 62–78.

———. *Violence in Republican Rome.* Oxford, 1968. (Reissued with new introduction, 1999.)

———. *Cicero as Evidence: A Historian's Companion.* Oxford, 2008.

MacKendrick, P. *The Philosophical Books of Cicero.* New York, 1989.

———. *The Speeches of Cicero.* London, 1995.

May, J. M. "The *Ethica Digressio* and Cicero's *Pro Milone:* A Progression of Intensity from *Logos* to *Ethos* to *Pathos*." *Classical Journal* 74 (1979): 240–46.

———. "The Image of the Ship of State in Cicero's *Pro Sestio*." *Maia* 3 (1980): 259–64.

———. *Trials of Character: The Eloquence of Ciceronian Ethos.* Chapel Hill and London, 1988.

———. "Cicero's *Pro Milone*: An Ideal Speech of an Ideal Orator." In *The Orator in Action and Theory in Greece and Rome* (*Studies in Honor of George A Kennedy*), edited by C. W. Wooten, 123–34. Mnemosyne Supplement, 225. Leiden, 2001.

———, ed. *Brill's Companion to Cicero: Oratory and Rhetoric.* Leiden, 2002.

May, J. M., and J. Wisse. *Cicero, On the Ideal Orator.* New York, Oxford, 2001.

Millar, F. *The Crowd in Rome in the Late Republic.* Jerome Lectures, 22. Ann Arbor, 1998.

Mitchell, T. N. *Cicero: The Ascending Years.* New Haven, 1979.

——. *Cicero, the Senior Statesman.* New Haven, 1991.

Morstein-Marx, R. *Mass Oratory and Political Power in the Late Roman Republic.* Cambridge, 2004.

Porter, W. M. "Cicero's *Pro Archia* and the Responsibilities of Reading." *Rhetorica* 8 (1990): 137–52.

Powell, J. G. F., ed. *Cicero the Philosopher.* Oxford, 1995.

——, ed. *Cicero,* Laelius, On Friendship (Laelius de Amicitia) *and the* Dream of Scipio (Somnium Scipionis). Warminster, 1990.

Powell, J. G. F., and J. Paterson, eds. *Cicero the Advocate.* Oxford, 2004.

Rawson, E. *Cicero: A Portrait.* Ithaca, 1983.

——. *Intellectual Life in the Late Roman Republic.* Baltimore, 1985.

Riggsby, A. M. *Crime and Community in Ciceronian Rome.* Austin, 1999.

Ruebel, J. S. "The Trial of Milo in 52 B.C.: A Chronological Study." *Transactions of the American Philological Association* 109 (1979): 231–49.

Steele, C. E. W. *Cicero, Rhetoric, and Empire.* Oxford, 2001.

——. *Reading Cicero: Genre and Performance in Late Republican Rome.* London, 2005.

Stockton, D. *Cicero, A Political Biography.* New York, 1971.

Tatum, W. J. "Cicero and the *Bona Dea* Scandal." *Classical Philology* 85 (1990): 202–8.

——. *The Patrician Tribune: Publius Clodius Pulcher.* Chapel Hill and London, 1999.

Taylor, L. R. *Party Politics in the Age of Caesar.* Berkeley, 1949.

Treggiari, S. "Home and Forum: Cicero Between 'Public' and 'Private.'" *Transactions of the American Philological Association* 128 (1998): 1–23.

Vasaly, A. *Representations: Images of the World in Ciceronian Oratory.* Berkeley, Los Angeles, Oxford, 1993.

Wisse, J. *Ethos and Pathos from Aristotle to Cicero.* Amsterdam, 1989.

———. "The Intellectual Background of Cicero's Rhetorical Works." In *Brill's Companion to Cicero: Oratory and Rhetoric*, edited by J. M. May, 331–74. Leiden, 2002.

———. "The Riddle of the *Pro Milone:* The Rhetoric of Rational Argument." In *Logos: Rational Argument in Classical Rhetoric*, edited by J. Powell, 35–68. London, 2007.

Wood, N. *Cicero's Social and Political Thought*. Berkeley, Los Angeles, London, 1988.

Latin Text

De inventione 1.1

[1] Saepe et multum hoc mecum cogitavi, bonine an mali plus attulerit hominibus et civitatibus copia dicendi ac summum eloquentiae studium. Nam cum et nostrae rei publicae detrimenta considero et maximarum civitatum veteres animo calamitates colligo, non minimam video per disertissimos homines invectam partem incommodorum; cum autem res ab nostra memoria propter vetustatem remotas ex litterarum monumentis repetere instituo, multas urbes constitutas, plurima bella restincta, firmissimas societates, sanctissimas amicitias intellego cum animi ratione tum facilius eloquentia comparatas. Ac me quidem diu cogitantem ratio ipsa in hanc potissimum sententiam ducit, ut existimem sapientiam sine eloquentia parum prodesse civitatibus, eloquentiam vero sine sapientia nimium obesse plerumque, prodesse nunquam. Quare si quis omissis rectissimis atque honestissimis studiis rationis et offici consumit omnem operam in exercitatione dicendi, is inutilis sibi, perniciosus patriae civis alitur; qui vero ita sese armat

eloquentia, ut non oppugnare commoda patriae, sed pro his propugnare possit, is mihi vir et suis et publicis rationibus utilissimus atque amicissimus civis fore videtur.

In Catilinam 2.22–25

[22] Postremum autem genus est non solum numero verum etiam genere ipso atque vita quod proprium Catilinae est, de eius dilectu, immo vero de complexu eius ac sinu; quos pexo capillo, nitidos, aut imberbis aut bene barbatos videtis, manicatis et talaribus tunicis, velis amictos, non togis; quorum omnis industria vitae et vigilandi labor in antelucanis cenis expromitur. [23] In his gregibus omnes aleatores, omnes adulteri, omnes impuri impudicique versantur. Hi pueri tam lepidi ac delicati non solum amare et amari neque saltare et cantare sed etiam sicas vibrare et spargere venena didicerunt. Qui nisi exeunt, nisi pereunt, etiam si Catilina perierit, scitote hoc in re publica seminarium Catilinarum futurum. Verum tamen quid sibi isti miseri volunt? num suas secum mulierculas sunt in castra ducturi? Quem ad modum autem illis carere poterunt, his praesertim iam noctibus? Quo autem pacto illi Appenninum atque illas pruinas ac nivis perferent? Nisi idcirco se facilius hiemem toleraturos putant, quod nudi in conviviis saltare didicerunt.

[24] O bellum magno opere pertimescendum, cum hanc sit

habiturus Catilina scortorum cohortem praetoriam! Instruite nunc, Quirites, contra has tam praeclaras Catilinae copias vestra praesidia vestrosque exercitus. Et primum gladiatori illi confecto et saucio consules imperatoresque vestros opponite; deinde contra illam naufragorum eiectam ac debilitatam manum florem totius Italiae ac robur educite. Iam vero urbes coloniarum ac municipiorum respondebunt Catilinae tumulis silvestribus. Neque ego ceteras copias, ornamenta, praesidia vestra cum illius latronis inopia atque egestate conferre debeo. Sed si, omissis his rebus quibus nos suppeditamur, eget ille, senatu, equitibus Romanis, urbe, aerario, vectigalibus, cuncta Italia, provinciis omnibus, exteris nationibus, si his rebus omissis causas ipsas quae inter se confligunt contendere velimus, ex eo ipso quam valde illi iaceant intellegere possumus. Ex hac enim parte pudor pugnat, illinc petulantia; hinc pudicitia, illinc stuprum; hinc fides, illinc fraudatio; hinc pietas, illinc scelus; hinc constantia, illinc furor; hinc honestas, illinc turpitudo; hinc continentia, illinc libido; hinc denique aequitas, temperantia, fortitudo, prudentia, virtutes omnes certant cum iniquitate, luxuria, ignavia, temeritate, cum vitiis omnibus; postremo copia cum egestate, bona ratio cum perdita, mens sana cum amentia, bona denique spes cum omnium rerum desperatione confligit. In eius modi certamine ac proelio nonne, si hominum studia deficiant, di ipsi immortales cogant ab his praeclarissimis virtutibus tot et tanta vitia superari?

~ *Pro Archia poeta* 12–16

[12] Quaeres a nobis, Gratti, cur tanto opere hoc homine delectemur. Quia suppeditat nobis ubi et animus ex hoc forensi strepitu reficiatur et aures convicio defessae conquiescant. An tu existimas aut suppetere nobis posse quod cotidie dicamus in tanta varietate rerum, nisi animos nostros doctrina excolamus, aut ferre animos tantam posse contentionem, nisi eos doctrina eadem relaxemus? Ego vero fateor me his studiis esse deditum. Ceteros pudeat, si qui ita se litteris abdiderunt ut nihil possint ex eis neque ad communem adferre fructum neque in aspectum lucemque proferre; me autem quid pudeat qui tot annos ita vivo, iudices, ut a nullius umquam me tempore aut commodo aut otium meum abstraxerit aut voluptas avocarit aut denique somnus retardarit? [13] Qua re quis tandem me reprehendat, aut quis mihi iure suscenseat, si, quantum ceteris ad suas res obeundas, quantum ad festos dies ludorum celebrandos, quantum ad alias voluptates et ad ipsam requiem animi et corporis conceditur temporum, quantum alii tribuunt tempestivis conviviis, quantum denique alveolo, quantum pilae, tantum mihi egomet ad haec studia recolenda sumpsero? Atque id eo mihi concedendum est magis quod ex his studiis haec quoque crescit oratio et facultas quae, quantacumque est in me, numquam amicorum periculis defuit. Quae si cui levior videtur, illa quidem certe quae summa sunt ex quo fonte hauriam sentio. [14] Nam nisi multorum praeceptis multisque litteris mihi ab adulescentia suasissem nihil esse in vita magno opere expetendum nisi laudem atque honestatem, in ea

autem persequenda omnis cruciatus corporis, omnia pericula mortis atque exsili parvi esse ducenda, numquam me pro salute vestra in tot ac tantas dimicationes atque in hos profligatorum hominum cotidianos impetus obiecissem. Sed pleni omnes sunt libri, plenae sapientium voces, plena exemplorum vetustas; quae iacerent in tenebris omnia, nisi litterarum lumen accederet. Quam multas nobis imagines non solum ad intuendum verum etiam ad imitandum fortissimorum virorum expressas scriptores et Graeci et Latini reliquerunt! quas ego mihi semper in administranda re publica proponens animum et mentem meam ipsa cogitatione hominum excellentium conformabam.

[15] Quaeret quispiam: 'quid? illi ipsi summi viri quorum virtutes litteris proditae sunt istane doctrina quam tu effers laudibus eruditi fuerunt?' Difficile est hoc de omnibus confirmare, sed tamen est certum quid respondeam. Ego multos homines excellenti animo ac virtute fuisse sine doctrina, et naturae ipsius habitu prope divino per se ipsos et moderatos et gravis exstitisse fateor; etiam illud adiungo, saepius ad laudem atque virtutem naturam sine doctrina quam sine natura valuisse doctrinam. Atque idem ego hoc contendo, cum ad naturam eximiam et inlustrem accesserit ratio quaedam conformatioque doctrinae, tum illud nescio quid praeclarum ac singulare solere exsistere. [16] Ex hoc esse hunc numero quem patres nostri viderunt, divinum hominem, Africanum, ex hoc C. Laelium, L. Furium, moderatissimos homines et continentissimos, ex hoc fortissimum virum et illis temporibus doctissimum, M. Catonem illum senem; qui

profecto si nihil ad percipiendam colendamque virtutem litteris adiuvarentur, numquam se ad earum studium contulissent. Quod si non hic tantus fructus ostenderetur, et si ex his studiis delectatio sola peteretur, tamen, ut opinor, hanc animi remissionem humanissimam ac liberalissimam iudicaretis. Nam ceterae neque temporum sunt neque aetatum omnium neque locorum; at haec studia adulescentiam acuunt, senectutem oblectant, secundas res ornant, adversis perfugium ac solacium praebent, delectant domi, non impediunt foris, pernoctant nobiscum, peregrinantur, rusticantur.

~ *Ad familiares* 14.1

[1] *Scr. Dyrrhachi a.d.* vi *K. Dec. a 696 (58)*

TVLLIVS TERENTIAE SVAE, TVLLIOLAE SVAE,

CICERONI SVO S. D.

Et litteris multorum et sermone omnium perfertur ad me incredibilem tuam virtutem et fortitudinem esse teque nec animi neque corporis laboribus defatigari. Me miserum! te ista virtute, fide, probitate, humanitate in tantas aerumnas propter me incidisse, Tulliolamque nostram, ex quo patre tantas voluptates capiebat, ex eo tantos percipere luctus! Nam quid ego de Cicerone dicam? Qui cum primum sapere coepit, acerbissimos dolores miseriasque percepit. Quae si, tu ut scribis, 'fato facta' putarem, ferrem paulo facilius; sed omnia sunt mea culpa commissa, qui ab iis me amari putabam qui invidebant, eos non sequebar qui petebant. [2] Quod si nostris consiliis usi essemus neque apud nos tantum valuisset sermo aut stultorum amicorum aut improborum, beatissimi viveremus. Nunc quoniam sperare nos amici iubent, dabo operam ne mea valetudo tuo labori desit. Res quanta sit intellego quantoque fuerit facilius manere domi quam redire; sed tamen si omnis tr. pl. habemus, si Lentulum tam studiosum quam videtur, si vero etiam Pompeium et Caesarem, non est desperandum.

[3] De familia quo modo placuisse scribis amicis faciemus. De loco nunc quidem iam abiit pestilentia, sed quam diu fuit me non attigit. Plancius, homo officiosissimus, me cupit esse secum et adhuc retinet. Ego volebam loco magis deserto esse in Epiro, quo neque Piso veniret nec milites, sed adhuc Plancius retinet; sperat posse fieri ut mecum in Italiam decedat. Quem ego diem si videro et si in vestrum complexum venero ac si et vos et me ipsum reciperaro, satis magnum mihi fructum videbor percepisse et vestrae pietatis et meae.

[4] Pisonis humanitas, virtus, amor in omnis nos tantus est, ut nihil supra possit. Utinam ea res ei voluptati sit! gloriae quidem video fore. De Quinto fratre nihil ego te accusavi, sed vos, cum praesertim tam pauci sitis, volui esse quam coniunctissimos. [5] Quibus me voluisti agere gratias egi et me a te certiorem factum esse scripsi. Quod ad me, mea Terentia, scribis te vicum vendituram, quid, obsecro te, me miserum! quid futurum est? et si nos premet eadem fortuna, quid puero misero fiet? Non queo relinqua scribere; tanta vis lacrimarum est; neque te

in eundem fletum adducam; tantum scribo: Si erunt in officio amici, pecunia non derit; si non erunt, tu efficere tua pecunia non poteris. Per fortunas miseras nostras, vide ne puerum perditum perdamus; cui si aliquid erit ne egeat, mediocri virtute opus est et mediocri fortuna ut cetera consequatur. [6] Fac valeas et ad me tabellarios mittas, ut sciam quid agatur et vos quid agatis. Mihi omnino iam brevis exspectatio est, Tulliolae et Ciceroni salutem dic. Valete. D. a.d. vi K. Decembr. Dyrrhachi.

[7] Dyrrhachium veni, quod et libera civitas est et in me officiosa et proxima Italiae; sed si offendet me loci celebritas, alio me conferam, ad te scribam.

Pro P. Sestio 45–46

[45] Unum autem mihi restabat illud quod forsitan non nemo vir fortis et acris animi magnique dixerit: 'restitisses, repugnasses, mortem pugnans oppetisses.' De quo te, te, inquam, patria, testor et vos, penates patriique dei, me vestrarum sedum templorumque causa, me propter salutem meorum civium, quae mihi semper fuit mea carior vita, dimicationem caedemque fugisse. Etenim si mihi in aliqua nave cum meis amicis naviganti hoc, iudices, accidisset, ut multi ex multis locis praedones classibus eam navem se oppressuros minitarentur nisi me unum sibi dedidissent, si id vectores negarent ac mecum simul interire quam me tradere hostibus mallent, iecissem ipse me potius in profundum, ut ceteros conservarem, quam illos mei tam cupidos non modo ad certam mortem, sed in magnum vitae discrimen adducerem.

[46] Cum vero in hanc rei publicae navem, ereptis senatui gubernaculis fluitantem in alto tempestatibus seditionum ac discordiarum, armatae tot classes, nisi ego essem unus deditus, incursurae viderentur, cum proscriptio, caedes, direptio denuntiaretur, cum alii me suspicione periculi sui non defenderent, alii vetere odio bonorum incitarentur, alii inviderent, alii obstare sibi me arbitrarentur, alii ulcisci dolorem aliquem suum vellent, alii rem ipsam publicam atque hunc bonorum statum otiumque odissent et ob hasce causas tot tamque varias me unum deposcerent, depugnarem potius cum summo non dicam exitio, sed periculo certe vestro liberorumque vestrorum, quam id quod omnibus impendebat unus pro omnibus susciperem ac subirem?

Ad Quintum fratrem 2.4

Scr. Romae medio mense Mart. an. 698 (56)

MARCVS QVINTO FRATRI SALVTEM

[1] Sestius noster absolutus est a. d. II Id. Mart. Et, quod vehementer interfuit rei publicae, nullam videri in eius modi causa dissensionem esse, omnibus sententiis absolutus est. Illud quod tibi curae saepe esse intellexeram, ne cui iniquo relinqueremus vituperandi locum qui nos ingratos esse diceret nisi illius perversitatem quibusdam in rebus quam humanissime ferremus, scito hoc nos in eo iudicio consecutos esse, ut omnium gratissimi iudicaremur; nam defendendo moroso homine cumulatissime satis fecimus et, id quod ille maxime

cupiebat, Vatinium, a quo palam oppugnabatur, arbitratu nostro concidimus dis hominibusque plaudentibus. Quin etiam Paulus noster, cum testis productus esset in Sestium, confirmavit se nomen Vatini delaturum si Macer Licinius cunctaretur, et Macer ab Sesti subselliis surrexit ac se illi non defuturum adfirmavit. Quid quaeris? Homo petulans et audax [Vatinius] valde perturbatus debilitatusque discessit.

[2] Quintus [filius] tuus, puer optimus, eruditur egregie; hoc nunc magis animum adverto, quod Tyrannio docet apud me. Domus utriusque nostrum aedificatur strenue; redemptori tuo dimidium pecuniae curavi; spero nos ante hiemem contubernalis fore. De nostra Tullia tui me hercule amantissima spero cum Crassipede nos confecisse; <sed> dies erant duo qui post Latinas habentur religiosi (ceterum confectum erat Latiar), <et> erat exiturus.

De oratore 1.16–20

[16] Quibus de causis quis non iure miretur ex omni memoria aetatum, temporum, civitatum tam exiguum oratorum numerum inveniri? Sed enim maius est hoc quiddam quam homines opinantur, et pluribus ex artibus studiisque conlectum. Quid enim quis aliud in maxima discentium multitudine, summa magistrorum copia, praestantissimis hominum ingeniis, infinita causarum varietate, amplissimis eloquentiae propositis praemiis esse causae putet, nisi rei quandam incredibilem magnitudinem ac difficultatem? [17] Est enim et scientia comprehendenda rerum plurimarum, sine qua verborum

volubilitas inanis atque inridenda est, et ipsa oratio conformanda non solum electione, sed etiam constructione verborum, et omnes animorum motus, quos hominum generi rerum natura tribuit, penitus pernoscendi, quod omnis vis ratioque dicendi in eorum qui audiunt mentibus aut sedandis aut excitandis expromenda est; accedat eodem oportet lepos quidam facetiaeque et eruditio libero digna celeritasque et brevitas et respondendi et lacessendi subtili venustate atque urbanitate coniuncta; [18] tenenda praeterea est omnis antiquitas exemplorumque vis, neque legum ac iuris civilis scientia neglegenda est. Nam quid ego de actione ipsa plura dicam? Quae motu corporis, quae gestu, quae vultu, quae vocis conformatione ac varietate moderanda est: quae sola per se ipsa quanta sit, histrionum levis ars et scaena declarat; in qua cum omnes in oris et vocis et motus moderatione laborent, quis ignorat quam pauci sint fuerintque, quos animo aequo spectare possimus? Quid dicam de thesauro rerum omnium, memoria? Quae nisi custos inventis cogitatisque rebus et verbis adhibeatur, intellegimus omnia, etiam si praeclarissima fuerint in oratore, peritura. [19] Quam ob rem mirari desinamus, quae causa sit eloquentium paucitatis, cum ex eis rebus universis eloquentia constet, in quibus singulis elaborare permagnum est, hortemurque potius liberos nostros ceterosque, quorum gloria nobis et dignitas cara est, ut animo rei magnitudinem complectantur neque eis aut praeceptis aut magistris aut exercitationibus, quibus utuntur omnes, sed aliis quibusdam se id quod expetunt, consequi posse confidant. [20] Ac mea quidem sententia nemo poterit esse omni laude cumulatus orator, nisi erit omnium rerum magnarum atque artium scientiam consecutus: etenim ex rerum cognitione efflorescat et redundet oportet oratio. Quae, nisi res est ab oratore percepta et cognita, inanem quandam habet elocutionem et paene puerilem.

❧ *Pro T. Annio Milone* 24–29

[24] P. Clodius, cum statuisset omni scelere in praetura vexare rem publicam videretque ita tracta esse comitia anno superiore ut non multos mensis praeturam gerere posset, qui non honoris gradum spectaret, ut ceteri, sed et L. Paulum conlegam effugere vellet, singulari virtute civem, et annum integrum ad dilacerandam rem publicam quaereret, subito reliquit annum suum seseque in proximum transtulit, non, ut fit, religione aliqua, sed ut haberet, quod ipse dicebat, ad praeturam gerendam, hoc est ad evertendam rem publicam, plenum annum atque integrum. [25] Occurrebat ei mancam ac debilem praeturam futuram suam consule Milone; eum porro summo consensu populi Romani consulem fieri videbat. Contulit se ad eius competitores, sed ita totam ut petitionem ipse solus etiam invitis illis gubernaret, tota ut comitia suis, ut dictitabat, umeris sustineret. Convocabat tribus, se interponebat, Collinam novam dilectu perditissimorum civium conscribebat. Quanto ille plura miscebat, tanto hic magis in dies convalescebat. Ubi vidit homo ad omne facinus paratissimus fortissimum virum, inimicissimum suum, certissimum consulem, idque intellexit non solum

sermonibus, sed etiam suffragiis populi Romani saepe esse declaratum, palam agere coepit et aperte dicere occidendum Milonem. [26] Servos agrestis et barbaros, quibus silvas publicas depopulatus erat Etruriamque vexarat, ex Appennino deduxerat, quos videbatis. Res erat minime obscura. Etenim dictitabat palam consulatum Miloni eripi non posse, vitam posse. Significavit hoc saepe in senatu, dixit in contione; quin etiam M. Favonio, fortissimo viro, quaerenti ex eo qua spe fureret Milone vivo, respondit triduo illum aut summum quadriduo esse periturum; quam vocem eius ad hunc M. Catonem statim Favonius detulit. [27] Interim cum sciret Clodius—neque enim erat id difficile scire a Lanuvinis—iter sollemne, legitimum, necessarium ante diem XIII Kalendas Februarias Miloni esse Lanuvium ad flaminem prodendum, quod erat dictator Lanuvi Milo, Roma subito ipse profectus pridie est ut ante fundum, quod re intellectum est, Miloni insidias conlocaret; atque ita profectus est ut contionem turbulentam in qua eius furor desideratus est, quae illo ipso die habita est, relinqueret, quam, nisi obire facinoris locum tempusque voluisset, numquam reliquisset. [28] Milo autem cum in senatu fuisset eo die quoad senatus est dimissus, domum venit, calceos et vestimenta mutavit, paulisper, dum se uxor, ut fit, comparat, commoratus est, dein profectus id temporis cum iam Clodius, si quidem eo die Romam venturus erat, redire potuisset. Obviam fit ei Clodius, expeditus, in equo, nulla raeda, nullis impedimentis, nullis Graecis comitibus, ut solebat, sine uxore quod numquam fere; cum hic insidiator, qui iter illud ad caedem faciendam apparasset, cum uxore veheretur in raeda, paenulatus, magno et impedito et muliebri ac delicato ancillarum puerorumque comitatu. [29] Fit obviam Clodio ante fundum eius hora fere undecima aut non multo secus. Statim complures cum telis in hunc faciunt de loco superiore impetum; adversi raedarium occidunt. Cum autem hic de raeda reiecta paenula desiluisset seque acri animo defenderet, illi qui erant cum Clodio gladiis eductis, partim recurrere ad raedam ut a tergo Milonem adorirentur, partim, quod hunc iam interfectum putarent, caedere incipiunt eius servos qui post erant; ex quibus qui animo fideli in dominum et praesenti fuerunt, partim occisi sunt, partim, cum ad raedam pugnari viderent, domino succurrere prohiberentur, Milonem occisum et ex ipso Clodio audirent et re vera putarent, fecerunt id servi Milonis—dicam enim aperte non derivandi criminis causa, sed ut factum est—nec imperante nec sciente nec praesente domino, quod suos quisque servos in tali re facere voluisset.

Ad familiares 16.4

Scr. Leucade vii *Id. Nov. a. 704 (50)*

TVLLIVS TIRONI SVO S. P. D. ET CICERO ET Q. FRATER ET Q. F.

[1] Varie sum adfectus tuis litteris, valde priore pagina perturbatus, paulum altera recreatus. Qua re nunc quidem non dubito quin, quoad plane valeas, te neque navigationi neque viae committas. Satis te mature videro, si plane

confirmatum videro. De medico et tu bene existimari scribis et ego sic audio; sed plane curationes eius non probo; ius enim dandum tibi non fuit, quom κακοστόμαχος esses. Sed tamen et ad illum scripsi accurate et ad Lysonem. [2] Ad Curium vero, suavissimum hominem et summi offici summaeque humanitatis, multa scripsi, in his etiam ut, si tibi videretur, te ad se traferret; Lyso enim noster vereor ne neglegentior sit, primum quia omnes Graeci, deinde quod, cum a me litteras accepisset, mihi nullas remisit. Sed eum tu laudas; tu igitur quid faciendum sit iudicabis. Illud, mi Tiro, te rogo sumptu ne parcas ulla in re, quod ad valetudinem opus sit. Scripsi ad Curium quod dixisses daret. Medico ipsi puto aliquid dandum esse, quo sit studiosior. [3] Innumerabilia tua sunt in me officia domestica, forensia, urbana, provincialia, in re privata, in publica, in studiis, in litteris nostris; omnia viceris, si, ut spero, te validum videro. Ego puto te bellissime, si recte erit, cum quaestore Mescinio decursurum. Non inhumanus est teque, ut mihi visus est, diligit. Et cum valetudini tuae diligentissime consulueris, tum, mi Tiro, consulito navigationi. Nulla in re iam te festinare volo; nihil laboro, nisi ut salvus sis. [4] Sic habeto, mi Tiro, neminem esse qui me amet quin idem te amet, et cum tua et mea maxime interest te valere, tum multis est curae. Adhuc dum mihi nullo loco deesse vis, numquam te confirmare potuisti; nunc te nihil impedit; omnia depone, corpori servi. Quantam diligentiam in valetudinem tuam contuleris, tanti me fieri a te iudicabo. Vale, mi Tiro, vale,

vale et salve. Lepta tibi salutem dicit et omnes. Vale. VII Id. Nov. Leucade.

~ *Ad familiares* 14.18

Scr. Formiis IX *K. Febr. a. 705 (49).*

TVLLIVS TERENTIAE SVAE ET PATER SVAVISSIMAE FILIAE, CICERO MATRI ET SORORI S. D. P.

[1] Considerandum vobis etiam atque etiam, animae meae, diligenter puto quid faciatis, Romaene sitis an mecum an aliquo tuto loco; id non solum meum consilium est sed etiam vestrum. Mihi veniunt in mentem haec, Romae vos esse tuto posse per Dolabellam, eamque rem posse nobis adiumento esse, si quae vis aut si quae rapinae fieri coeperint. Sed rursus illud me movet, quod video omnis bonos abesse Roma et eos mulieres suas secum habere. Haec autem regio, in qua ego sum, nostrorum est cum oppidorum tum etiam praediorum, ut et multum esse mecum et, cum abieritis, commode et in nostris esse possitis. [2] Mihi plane non satis constat adhuc utrum sit melius. Vos videte quid aliae faciant isto loco feminae, et ne, cum velitis, exire non liceat. Id velim diligenter etiam atque etiam vobiscum et cum amicis consideretis. Domus ut propugnacula et praesidium habeat Philotimo dicetis; et velim tabellarios instituatis certos, ut cotidie aliquas a vobis litteras accipiam; maxime autem date operam ut valeatis, si nos vultis valere. VIIII K. Formiis.

~ *Ad familiares* 14.20

Scr. de Venusino K. Oct. a. 707 (47).

TVLLIVS S. D. TERENTIAE SVAE.

In Tusculanum nos venturos putamus aut Nonis aut postridie. Ibi ut sint omnia parata (plures enim fortasse nobiscum erunt et, ut arbitror, diutius ibi commorabimur); labrum si in balineo non est, ut sit, item cetera quae sunt ad victum et ad valetudinem necessaria. Vale. K. Oct. de Venusino.

~ *Brutus* 1–9

[1] Cum e Cilicia decedens Rhodum venissem et eo mihi de Q. Hortensi morte esset adlatum, opinione omnium maiorem animo cepi dolorem. Nam et amico amisso cum consuetudine iucunda tum multorum officiorum coniunctione me privatum videbam et interitu talis auguris dignitatem nostri conlegi deminutam dolebam; qua in cogitatione et cooptatum me ab eo in conlegium recordabar, in quo iuratus iudicium dignitatis meae fecerat, et inauguratum ab eodem, ex quo augurum institutis in parentis eum loco colere debebam. [2] Augebat etiam molestiam quod magna sapientium civium bonorumque penuria vir egregius coniunctissimusque mecum consiliorum omnium societate alienissimo rei publicae tempore exstinctus et auctoritatis et prudentiae suae triste nobis desiderium reliquerat, dolebamque quod non, ut plerique putabant, adversarium aut

obtrectatorem laudum mearum sed socium potius et consortem gloriosi laboris amiseram. [3] Etenim si in leviorum artium studio memoriae proditum est poetas nobilis poetarum aequalium morte doluisse, quo tandem animo eius interitum ferre debui, cum quo certare erat gloriosius quam omnino adversarium non habere? Cum praesertim non modo numquam sit aut illius a me cursus impeditus aut ab illo meus, sed contra semper alter ab altero adiutus et communicando et monendo et favendo. [4] Sed quoniam perpetua quadam felicitate usus ille excessit e vita suo magis quam suorum civium tempore et tum occidit cum lugere facilius rem publicam posset, si viveret, quam iuvare, vixitque tam diu quam licuit in civitate bene beateque vivere: nostro incommodo detrimentoque, si est ita necesse, doleamus, illius vero mortis opportunitatem benevolentia potius quam misericordia prosequamur, ut, quotienscumque de clarissimo et beatissimo viro cogitemus, illum potius quam nosmet ipsos diligere videamur. [5] Nam si id dolemus, quod eo iam frui nobis non licet, nostrum est id malum quod modice feramus, ne id non ad amicitiam sed ad domesticam utilitatem referre videamur; sin tamquam illi ipsi acerbitatis aliquid acciderit angimur, summam eius felicitatem non satis grato animo interpretamur.

[6] Etenim si viveret Q. Hortensius, cetera fortasse desideraret una cum reliquis bonis et fortibus civibus, hunc autem aut praeter ceteros aut cum paucis sustineret dolorem, cum forum populi Romani, quod fuisset quasi theatrum

illius ingeni, voce erudita et Romanis Graecisque auribus digna spoliatum atque orbatum videret. [7] Equidem angor animo non consili, non ingeni, non auctoritatis armis egere rem publicam, quae didiceram tractare quibusque me assuefeceram quaeque erant propria cum praestantis in re publica viri tum bene moratae et bene constitutae civitatis. Quod si fuit in re publica tempus ullum, cum extorquere arma posset e manibus iratorum civium boni civis auctoritas et oratio, tum profecto fuit cum patrocinium pacis exclusum est aut errore hominum aut timore. [8] Ita nobismet ipsis accidit ut, quamquam essent multo magis alia lugenda, tamen hoc doleremus quod, quo tempore aetas nostra perfuncta rebus amplissimis tamquam in portum confugere deberet non inertiae neque desidiae, sed oti moderati atque honesti, cumque ipsa oratio iam nostra canesceret haberetque suam quandam maturitatem et quasi senectutem, tum arma sunt ea sumpta, quibus illi ipsi, qui didicerant eis uti gloriose, quem ad modum salutariter uterentur, non reperiebant. [9] Itaque ei mihi videntur fortunate beateque vixisse cum in ceteris civitatibus tum maxime in nostra, quibus cum auctoritate rerumque gestarum gloria tum etiam sapientiae laude perfrui licuit. Quorum memoria et recordatio in maximis nostris gravissimisque curis iucunda sane fuit, cum in eam nuper ex sermone quodam incidissemus.

De amicitia 19–23

[19] Sic enim mihi perspicere videor, ita natos esse nos ut inter omnes esset societas quaedam, maior autem ut quisque proxime accederet; itaque cives potiores quam peregrini, propinqui quam alieni; cum his enim amicitiam natura ipsa peperit, sed ea non satis habet firmitatis; namque hoc praestat amicitia propinquitati, quod ex propinquitate benevolentia tolli potest, ex amicitia non potest; sublata enim benevolentia amicitiae nomen tollitur, propinquitatis manet. [20] Quanta autem vis amicitiae sit, ex hoc intellegi maxime potest, quod ex infinita societate generis humani, quam conciliavit ipsa natura, ita contracta res est et adducta in angustum, ut omnis caritas aut inter duos aut inter paucos iungeretur. Est enim amicitia nihil aliud nisi omnium divinarum humanarumque rerum cum benevolentia et caritate consensio; qua quidem haud scio an excepta sapientia nihil melius homini sit a dis immortalibus datum. Divitias alii praeponunt, bonam alii valetudinem, alii potentiam, alii honores, multi etiam voluptates: beluarum hoc quidem extremum; illa autem superiora caduca et incerta, posita non tam in consiliis nostris quam in fortunae temeritate. Qui autem in virtute summum bonum ponunt, praeclare illi quidem, sed haec ipsa virtus amicitiam et gignit et continet, nec sine virtute amicitia esse ullo pacto potest. [21] Iam virtutem ex consuetudine vitae sermo-

nisque nostri interpretemur, nec eam, ut quidam docti, verborum magnificentia metiamur, virosque bonos eos qui habentur numeremus: Paulos, Catones, Galos, Scipiones, Philos. His communis vita contenta est, eos autem omittamus qui omnino nusquam reperiuntur.

[22] Tales igitur inter viros amicitia tantas opportunitates habet quantas vix queo dicere. Principio, qui potest esse vita vitalis, ut ait Ennius, quae non in amici mutua benevolentia conquiescat? Quid dulcius quam habere quicum omnia audeas sic loqui ut tecum? Qui esset tantus fructus in prosperis rebus nisi haberes qui illis aeque ac tu ispe gauderet? Adversas vero ferre difficile esset sine eo qui illas gravius etiam quam tu ferret. Denique ceterae res quae expetuntur opportunae sunt singulae rebus fere singulis: divitiae ut utare, opes ut colare, honores ut laudere, voluptates ut gaudeas, valetudo ut dolore careas et muneribus fungare corporis. Amicitia res plurimas continet, quoquo te verteris praesto est, nullo loco excluditur, numquam intempestiva, numquam molesta est. Itaque non aqua, non igni, ut aiunt, locis pluribus utimur quam amicitia (neque ego nunc de vulgari aut de mediocri, quae tamen ipsa et delectat et prodest, sed de vera et perfecta loquor, qualis eorum qui pauci nominantur fuit); nam et secundas res splendidiores facit amicitia, et adversas partiens communicansque leviores.

[23] Cumque plurimas et maximas commoditates amicitia continet, tum illa nimirum praestat omnibus, quod bonam spem praelucet in posterum, nec debilitari animos aut cadere patitur. Verum enim amicum qui intuetur, tamquam exemplar aliquod intuetur sui. Quocirca et absentes adsunt, et egentes abundant et imbecilli valent, et quod difficilius dictu est, mortui vivunt: tantus eos honos, memoria, desiderium prosequitur amicorum, ex quo illorum beata mors videtur, horum vita laudabilis. Quod si exemeris ex rerum natura benevolentiae iunctionem, nec domus ulla nec urbs stare poterit, nec agri quidem cultus permanebit. Id si minus intellegitur, quanta vis amicitiae concordiaeque sit ex dissensionibus atque discordiis percipi potest. Quae enim domus tam stabilis, quae tam firma civitas est, quae non odiis atque discidiis funditus possit everti? Ex quo quantum boni sit in amicitia iudicari potest.

De officiis 1.134–137

[134] Sit ergo hic sermo, in quo Socratici maxime excellent, lenis minimeque pertinax, insit in eo lepos. Nec vero, tamquam in possessionem suam venerit, excludat alios, sed cum reliquis in rebus tum in sermone communi vicissitudinem non iniquam putet. Ac videat in primis quibus de rebus loquatur: si seriis, severitatem adhibeat, si iocosis, leporem. In primisque provideat ne sermo vitium aliquod indicet inesse in moribus; quod maxime tum solet

evenire cum studiose de absentibus detrahendi causa aut per ridiculum aut severe maledice contumelioseque dicitur. [135] Habentur autem plerumque sermones aut de domesticis negotiis aut de re publica aut de artium studiis atque doctrina. Danda igitur opera est ut, etiamsi aberrare ad alia coeperit, ad haec revocetur oratio, sed †utcumque aderunt†; neque enim isdem de rebus nec omni tempore nec similiter delectamur. Animadvertendum est etiam quatenus sermo delectationem habeat, et ut incipiendi ratio fuerit, ita sit desinendi modus.

[136] Sed quomodo in omni vita rectissime praecipitur ut perturbationes fugiamus, id est motus animi nimios rationi non optemperantes, sic eiusmodi motibus sermo debet vacare, ne aut ira exsistat aut cupiditas aliqua aut pigritia aut ignavia aut tale aliquid appareat, maximeque curandum est ut eos quibuscum sermonem conferemus et vereri et diligere videamur. Obiurgationes etiam nonnumquam incidunt necessariae, in quibus utendum est fortasse et vocis contentione maiore et verborum gravitate acriore, id agendum etiam, ut ea facere videamur irati. Sed ut ad urendum et secandum, sic ad hoc genus castigandi raro invitique veniemus, nec umquam nisi necessario, si nulla reperietur alia medicina; sed tamen ira procul absit, cum qua nihil recte fieri, nihil considerate potest. [137] Magnam autem partem clementi castigatione licet uti, gravitate tamen adiuncta, ut et severitas adhibeatur et contumelia repellatur, atque etiam illud ipsum quod acerbitatis habet obiurgatio, significandum est ipsius id causa

qui obiurgetur esse susceptum. Rectum est autem etiam in illis contentionibus quae cum inimicissimis fiunt, etiam si nobis indigna audiamus, tamen gravitatem retinere, iracundiam pellere; quae enim cum aliqua perturbatione fiunt, ea nec constanter fieri possunt neque iis qui adsunt probari. Deforme etiam est de se ipsum praedicare, falsa praesertim, et cum inrisione audientium imitari militem gloriosum.

Commentary

❧ *De inventione* 1.1

This selection begins the preface to Cicero's first published work, *De inventione*. While still a teenager of sixteen or eighteen years, Cicero began work on a rhetorical handbook that was originally intended to cover the five traditional *officia* ("activities") of the orator, viz., invention ("discovering" or thinking out the material), arrangement (ordering it), style (putting the ordered material into words), memory (memorizing the speech), and delivery (voice and gesture employed in delivering the speech). In the end, he completed only the two-book section on invention (hence the name of the treatise). Thirty-five years later, looking back on the handbook from the vantage point of being Rome's most successful orator, Cicero referred to *De inventione* as "the sketchy and unsophisticated work that found its way out of my notebooks when I was a boy, or rather a youth" (*De oratore* 1.5). Yet, ironically, it was the preface to *De inventione*, and particularly this section of it, that became one of late antiquity's most famous passages (cf. e.g., St. Augustine's use of it in *De doctrina Christiana*); it continued to be quoted throughout the Middle Ages and Renaissance.

In these opening sentences, young Cicero ponders the relationship between *sapientia* and *eloquentia* (wisdom and eloquence, i.e., philosophy and rhetoric), and poses the interesting and controversial question of whether eloquence has done more good or harm to humans and their communities. The question reveals Cicero's knowledge of, and interest in, the historic quarrel between philosophy and rhetoric, a quarrel that appears to have begun almost simultaneously with their emergence as disciplines (along with educational programs and institutions to support them). The preface of *De inventione* represents Cicero's initial attempt at reconciliation, a topic that will find a much more comprehensive treatment in his masterful treatise on the ideal orator, *De oratore*, published in 55 BCE (see below, pp. 53–58).

1 **multum** adverbial

-ne . . . an introduces an indirect question.

1-2 **boni . . . mali** partitive gens., dependent on *plus*

2 **attulerit** Note sing. verb with compound subject (*copia . . . ac . . . studium*, lines 2–3).

copia dicendi "fluency of speech"

4 **et . . . et** "both . . . and"

5 **animo** Construe with *colligo.*

6–7 **non minimam . . . partem** an example of the rhetorical device, LITOTES, by which the writer or speaker affirms something by denying or negating its opposite

6 **disertissimos** *Disertus* is often translated as "eloquent," but Cicero maintains a rather strict distinction in his writings between someone who is *disertus* and someone who is *eloquens*; translate *disertissimos* here as "very fluent/very skilled in speech."

invectam sc. *esse*; pf. pass. infinitive in indirect discourse, introduced by *video*

7–8 **ab nostra memoria** dependent upon the pple. *remotas*, which modifies *res* (line 7)

8–9 **ex litterarum monumentis** "in the annals/records of literature"; construe closely with *repetere* (line 9).

10–12 **constitutas . . . restincta . . . comparatas** sc. *esse*; infinitives in indirect discourse; note the lack of connectives joining these phrases, a rhetorical device known as ASYNDETON.

11-12 **cum . . . tum** "both . . . and"; *ratione* and *eloquentia* = abl. of means

13 **cogitantem** pple., modifying *me* (line 12)

potissimum adverbial, "chiefly, especially"

14-16 **sapientiam sine eloquentia . . . eloquentiam . . . sine . . . sapientia** The ideal, of course, is an orator and statesmen who is in possession of both wisdom and eloquence; more than thirty years later, Cicero will develop the portrait of such an orator in his magisterial dialogue, *De oratore* (see below, pp. 53–58).

15-16 **prodesse** and **obesse** are both compounds of *sum* and govern the dat. case; note the play on words, a rhetorical device whose technical name is PARONOMASIA.

16 **plerumque** adverbial, "for the most part, generally"

17 **si quis** = *si aliquis*

17-18 **omissis . . . studiis rationis et offici** abl. absolute

18 **rationis et offici** "rational thinking (i.e., philosophy) and moral duty/conduct"

19-20 **is . . . civis alitur** "this (man) is reared/nurtured as a citizen . . ."; *inutilis sibi* and *perniciosus patriae* are both adj. + dat. combinations modifying *civis*; note the striking and effective contrast with this citizen and the *civis* in line 23.

20 **vero** "but"

21 **eloquentia** abl. of means

21-22 **oppugnare . . . propugnare** another example of PARONOMASIA; cf. above, line 16, *obesse . . . prodesse*

22-23 **et suis et publicis rationibus** dat. after *utilissimus atque amicissimus*; translate "both to his own interests/affairs and those of his community."

24 **fore** = *futurum esse*

In Catilinam 2.22–25

Toward the end of his term as consul (63 BCE), Cicero uncovered a secret plot to overthrow the state; the conspiracy was led by Lucius Sergius Catilina, a nobly born but disenchanted and unscrupulous senator, who had been rebuffed in the consular elections two years running. After thwarting an assassination attempt during the morning call (*salutatio*) on November 7, Cicero convened a meeting of the Senate for the next day in the Temple of Jupiter Stator—a meeting that Catiline himself was so bold as to attend. On that occasion, Cicero delivered perhaps his most famous oration (known to posterity as the *First Oration against Catiline*), an oratorical tour de force in which he repeatedly urges the conspirator to leave Rome and join his revolutionary army. On the following day, November 9, at a public meeting in the forum, Cicero gave a second speech on the subject, a sharp invective in which he vividly characterizes Catiline and his followers and those loyal Romans who oppose them. Through the skillful use of character description (rhetorical ethos), Cicero paints a starkly contrasting portrait of good versus evil, of the honorable, upright Roman ideal versus its un-Roman antithesis. About halfway into the speech, Cicero identifies and describes six groups or types of men who comprise Catiline's revolutionary force; this selection begins with the description of the sixth and final group, Catiline's very own, "last not only in order but also in character and manner of life."

1 [22] **postremum** "last" and "lowest"; both senses are applicable here.

2 **genere** "in character"

2–3 **quod proprium Catilinae est** *Catilinae* is gen.; "one that is Catiline's own"

3 **immo vero** "in fact"

3–4 **de complexu . . . sinu** i.e., composed of his most intimate friends, his "bosom buddies"

4 **pexo capillo** abl. of description or quality

nitidos refers to the perfumes and oils with which they dressed their hair.

4–5 **imberbis aut bene barbatos** i.e., either beardless (because of their youth or effeminancy) or with full beards (because of their slovenliness or affectation); in this era, adult Roman males customarily went clean-shaven, except in times of mourning.

5 **manicatis et talaribus tunicis** In Cicero's day, a man's tunic (the loose-fitting garment worn under the toga) was typically short-sleeved and knee-length; to dress like a woman, in a full-length tunic with long sleeves, was considered effeminate.

5–6 **velis . . . non togis** It was considered indecorous for men to wear togas that were excessively wide and full; Catiline's dandies wear togas that look like sails!

6 **industria vitae et vigilandi labor** Note the artistic ordering of words and cases in an ABBA order (nominative, genitive, genitive, nominative), the rhetorical device known as CHIASMUS; *industria vitae* and *labor vigilandi* usually characterize the efforts of loyal citizens like Cicero, who have used their energies to work their way to prominence in the state; here Catiline's followers have perverted such virtues, wasting their efforts in banquets that last until dawn.

7 [23] **gregibus** literally "herds," i.e., gang; the word implies the sub-human nature of Catiline's friends.

9–10 **non solum . . . neque . . . sed etiam** "not only . . . nor . . . but also"

10 **saltare et cantare** activities that were, in general, considered beneath the dignity of a true Roman

11 **spargere venena** i.e., adding poisons to food or drink, a convenient method of eliminating one's rivals or enemies

qui nisi . . . The rel. pron. *qui* is not only the subject of the *nisi*-clause, but also refers to an antecedent (*pueri*, line 9) in the previous sentence (hence its placement at the start of the sentence); English in this case would use a demonstrative: "Unless these . . ."

12 **scitote** In classical Latin, the fut. imperative of *scio* is used in place of the pres.

hoc sing., agreeing with *seminarium*

Catilinarum Note the pl.

13 **futurum** = *futurum esse*

verum "yet"

13–14 **isti miseri** "such wretches"

14 **num** interrog. particle introducing a question that expects a negative answer; "certainly they are not going to lead . . . ?"

mulierculas Note the use of the diminutive, here to express contempt.

15 **quem ad modum** "how?"

16 **Appenninum** the mountain chain of the Appennines, near Etruria, where Manlius, Catiline's associate, had established his camp

17 **idcirco** explained by the *quod*-clause in line 18

18 **toleraturos** = *toleraturos esse*

20 [24] **o bellum magno opere pertimescendum** ironical

magno opere sometimes written as one word; used adverbially as an adv. of *magnus*, "greatly, very much"

20–21 **sit habiturus** the so-called periphrastic fut. subjunctive; translate as simple fut.

21 **cohortem praetoriam** i.e., the general's bodyguard

instruite A remarkable passage of rhetorical comparison begins here and extends through the end of this selection.

22 **Quirites** originally, the inhabitants of the Sabine town Cures; after the unification of the Romans and the Sabines, the name was used to denote the citizens of Rome in their civil capacity.

23 **praesidia . . . exercitus** The former indicates "garrisons" stationed in defense of cities and towns; the latter, armies in the field.

24 **gladiatori** referring contemptuously to Catiline

25 **eiectam** "stranded"; in keeping with the image contained in *naufragorum*

25-26 Note the word order, with its powerful juxtaposition of Catiline's *naufragorum manum* and *florem totius Italiae.*

27 **coloniarum ac municipiorum** Originally *coloniae* were settlements of Roman citizens, while *municipia* were Italian communities; following the War with the Allies (91–88) both groups enjoyed Roman citizenship and right of self-government.

28 **tumulis silvestribus** The haunts and rallying places for Catiline's band are in sharp contrast to the normal fortifications associated with cities (*urbes*, line 27).

30 **conferre** "compare"

omissis his rebus abl. absolute; *rebus* looks ahead to the items listed in lines 31–33 *senatu, equitibus . . .*

quibus abl. of means, with *suppeditamur* (line 31)

31 **nos suppeditamur, eget ille** Again, note the stark contrast, underlined by the very meaning of the verbs, as well as by the rhetorical CHIASMUS and ASYNDETON; *ille* refers to Catiline.

33 **his rebus omissis** reiterating, or rather restating the thought begun in line 30 with the abl. absolute

34 **contendere** here, "compare"

ex eo ipso i.e., by this very comparison

34-35 **quam . . . iaceant** literally, "how prostrate they lie," i.e., how greatly disadvantaged they are; indirect question, dependent upon *intellegere possumus*

35 **ex hac . . . parte** "on this side," contrasted with *illinc* (lines 36 ff.), "on that side"

38 **honestas** not "honesty"

39-40 **aequitas, temperantia, fortitudo, prudentia** With a small variation (*aequitas* for *iustitia*), Cicero lists the so-called four cardinal virtues, prominent in Platonic and Stoic thought.

42 **bona ratio** Cicero means to indicate here good or sound political thought, the hallmark of the *boni*, patriotic citizens, like-minded with Cicero and loyal to the government.

45 **nonne** expects an affirmative answer; the question is posed as a fut. less vivid condition: *si . . . deficiant . . . (nonne) di ipsi immortals cogant . . .* (lines 45–47).

46 **ab his praeclarissimis virtutibus** An abl. of means would be expected; Cicero seems to personify the virtues.

Pro Archia poeta 12–16

In the year following his consulship, Cicero was called upon to defend one of his former teachers and mentors, the poet A. Licinius Archias, in a case disputing Archias' claim to Roman citizenship. Archias, a Greek born in Syria, had come to Rome approximately forty years earlier. He had honored in his poetry the military accomplishments of one of Rome's foremost generals and politicians, Lucius Lucullus, who, in turn, became Archias' literary patron and eventual sponsor of his citizenship. In 62 BCE, a certain Grattius (perhaps backed by the powerful general and rival of Lucullus, Pompey the Great) charged the poet with having obtained Roman citizenship illegally. It is most likely that the charge was politically motivated, not so much aimed at Archias himself, but rather designed to embarrass and disgrace his patron Lucullus. Cicero's speech in defense of Archias is the shortest, and one of the most charming and influential, of his surviving orations. In the first half of the speech, the orator dispenses in workmanlike fashion with the legal charges concerning citizenship. He then devotes the rest of his oration to an *apologia* on behalf of liberal studies, in particular literary studies, arguing that even if Archias is not, in fact, a legal citizen, he should be, based on his contribution to arts, letters, and humanity in general. The passage excerpted below comprises the most famous portion of this section of the speech. It illustrates well Cicero's own, deeply held commitment to liberal studies, which will be reflected in many of his subsequent writings. Although we do not know definitively that Archias was acquitted, we are fairly safe in that assumption, seeing that Cicero subsequently in a private letter to one of his friends speaks as though Archias were still living in Rome. Coincidentally, Cicero's brother, Quintus, presided over Archias' trial as praetor.

1 [12] **Gratti** Grattius, the name of the prosecutor bringing the charge; note the vocative form of nouns ending in *-ius*.

tanto opere often written as one word; adv., "so greatly, so much"

2 **ubi** = *id quo*, "the means by which," referring to Archias' poetry; introduces a rel. clause of purpose

2–3 **et . . . et** "both . . . and"

3 **forensi** "of, or pertaining to the forum," here referring particularly to the law courts convened in the forum

convicio defessae participial phrase, modifying *aures; convicio* refers to the disputes and wrangling of the litigants and their legal counsel.

4 **an** here the equivalent of *num*, expecting a negative answer

suppetere "to be on hand, to be available to"; Cicero asserts that studying poetry and literature supplies him as an orator with much valuable material for the composition of his own speeches.

4–5 **quod . . . dicamus** The clause serves as the subject of *suppetere . . . posse* (line 4).

5 **cotidie . . . rerum** i.e., amid the daily activities in the forum

6–7 **excolamus; relaxemus** subjunctives in subordinate clauses within indirect discourse, or as in fut. less vivid conditions

6 **doctrina** abl. of means, as in line 7

aut the second alternative, following the first *aut* in line 4; *animos* is the subject of *ferre . . . posse.*

7 **eos** referring to *animos* (line 6)

doctrina eadem abl. of means

8 **ceteros pudeat** "let it shame others"; *pudeat* is jussive subjunctive

qui = *aliqui* (after *si*); refers to *ceteros*

9 **nihil** object of *adferre* and *proferre* (line 10)

9–10 **ad communem adferre fructum** i.e., by employing their studies for the common advantage, i.e., the benefit of the state

10 **in aspectum lucemque proferre** i.e., *in aspectum lucis*; the use of two nouns where we would expect a noun and an adj. or another modifier expressing a single idea is the rhetorical device called HENDIADYS (literally "one through two"); here Cicero refers to literary productivity. One's zeal for literature and its study should result either in a contribution to public life or in some literary accomplishment.

11 **me autem quid pudeat** "but why should it shame me"; note the contrast of *me* with *ceteros* (line 8); *pudeat* is deliberative subjunctive.

vivo Here the pres. tense has the force of the pres. pf.: "I have lived."

12–13 **aut . . . aut . . . aut . . . aut** The first *aut* connects *tempore* and *commodo*; the next three set out the three subjects/verbs of the result clause (introduced by *ita vivo*, line 11), all of which have as their direct object *me* (line 12); the piling up of such connectives is the rhetorical device known as POLYSYNDETON.

11–12 **a nullius . . .** Construe in this order: *a tempore aut commodo nullius*, "from the time (of peril) or interest of no one"; *tempus* in this context has a specialized meaning = *periculum*, i.e., "time of peril, need," referring especially to legal needs in criminal cases, in contrast to *commodum*, referring to civil cases. Cicero's point is that he has allowed nothing to interfere with his helping those who have been in need of his talents as an advocate.

12 **otium** here more than simply "leisure," but especially leisure time spent in literary pursuits and other study

13 **somnus** i.e., laziness, idleness

14–20 [13] This long question is actually a fut. more vivid condition, introduced by two potential subjunctives (*reprehendat, suscenseat*), replacing the expected fut. indicatives in the apodosis (i.e., conclusion) of the condition; the protasis (i.e., the if-clause) comes at the end of the question: *si . . . tantum* [*temporum*] *mihi egomet ad haec studia recolenda sumpsero*? The structure of the question is complicated by the insertion of a long correlative construction (*quantum . . . tantum*) containing six clauses (arranged in two tricolons, i.e., a series of three phrases or clauses), each introduced by the word *quantum* (thus employing also the rhetorical device known as ANAPHORA), followed finally by *tantum*, the resolution of the correlative construction and conclusion of the condition.

15–18 **quantum . . . temporum** "as much time as . . ."; *temporum* is partitive gen. and should be understood with each *quantum*; in the first tricolon of *quantum*-clauses, *quantum* is subject and *conceditur* (line 18) is the verb.

15 **ad . . . obeundas** Here and in lines 16 and 20, the gerundive + *ad* is used to show purpose.

16 **ludorum** Cicero refers here to the public games (*ludi*), celebrated usually in connection with religious festivals.

18–19 In this second tricolon, *quantum* [*temporum*] now becomes the object of *alii tribuunt.*

18 **tempestivis** "early"; dinners beginning earlier than usual were considered a sign of luxury and extravagance.

19 **pilae** Ball games were popular with the Romans, including forms of catch and a game that involved hitting a small, leather-covered ball against a wall, similar to modern-day handball.

19–20 **mihi egomet** Note the emphasis, as well as the contrast with *ceteris* (line 15), the same contrast noted in lines 8–11.

20–21 **eo . . . magis** "the more for this reason"; *eo* is explained by the *quod*-causal clause.

22 **oratio et facultas** HENDIADYS for *facultas oratoria*, "oratorical power"

quantacumque intended as self-deprecating: "however little"

23 **periculis** referring to the dangers of those under threat of criminal indictment; cf. *tempore* above (line 12); Cicero's oratorical ability has never failed his friends in need.

defuit takes the dat. case.

quae "this ability"; a connecting rel., where English would expect a demonstrative

si cui = *si alicui*

levior "rather trivial"

24–25 [14] **illa . . . sentio** The word order of these clauses, which flows well in Latin, presents difficulties for those who are used to English word order; *ex quo . . . hauriam* is an indirect question, introduced by *sentio* (line 25); construe in this order: *sentio ex quo fonte hauriam illa . . . quae summa sunt.*

24 **illa . . . quae summa sunt** In contrast to Cicero's *facultas oratoria*, which he describes as *levior* (line 23), this phrase refers to the highest ideals and principles of life; Cicero thus makes the point that both his oratorical abilities as well as those principles that guide his life and career (explicated in more detail in what follows) have been derived from his study of literature, philosophy, and the liberal arts.

25–31 [14] **nisi . . . obiecissem** *Nisi . . . suasissem* (lines 25–26) is the protasis of a contrary-to-fact, past condition that introduces two clauses in indirect discourse (*nihil esse . . . expedendum*, lines 26–27; and *omnis cruciatus . . . , omnia pericula . . . esse ducenda*, lines 28–29); *obiecissem* (line 31) is the verb of the apodosis or conclusion.

25 **praeceptis multisque litteris** abl. of means or instrument; translate *multis litteris* as "by extensive reading."

26 **mihi** object of *suasissem*

27 **nisi** Translate closely with *nihil* (line 26): "nothing but, nothing except . . ."

27–28 **in ea . . . persequenda** a gerundive: "in the pursuit of which," i.e., *laudem atque honestam*

29 **parvi esse ducenda** "ought to be considered of little importance"; *parvi* is gen. of price or value.

me object of *obiecissem* (line 31)

30–31 **dimicationes . . . impetus** referring to the conspiracy of Catiline in the previous year and the opposition presented to Cicero by the conspirator's followers

32 **pleni . . . plenae . . . plena** predicate adjs. modifying *libri*, *voces*, and *vetustas* respectively; note the ANAPHORA.

sapientium voces i.e., the pronouncements, or precepts of philosophers

exemplorum partitive gen., to be construed with all three instances of *plenus*; i.e., the examples of people whose lives have been guided and influenced by such principles

33 **quae . . . omnia** "all of which"; an example of a connecting rel., whose antecedent is *exemplorum* (line 32)

33–34 **nisi litterarum lumen accederet** i.e., if literature did not bring these great examples to light; note the metaphor.

34–36 **quam multas . . . imagines . . . fortissimorum virorum expressas** the object of *reliquerunt* (line 36) in this exclamatory sentence

36 **expressas** "clear, carefully modeled," describing *imagines* (line 34); note the metaphor; the language is descriptive of the work of a sculptor or artist. Cicero's point is that poetry and literature are monuments as lasting and formative as the portrait masks displayed in Roman houses, or the statues decorating public places.

scriptores nom.; its meaning is further specified by the addition of *et Graeci et Latini.*

37 **quas** a connecting rel. whose antecedent is *imagines* (line 34); object of *proponens* (line 38)

38 **ipsa cogitatione** abl. of means or instrument with *conformabam* (line 39)

40 [15] **quaeret quispiam 'quid . . . ?'** Cicero raises an imaginary objection, which he can then refute—a common oratorical tactic.

41 **litteris . . . istane doctrina** two abls. of means, the first to be taken with *proditae sunt*, the second with *eruditi fuerunt* (line 42)

42 **hoc** object of the infinitive *confirmare* (line 43), which acts as the subject of *difficile est*

44 **multos homines** subject of indirect discourse, introduced by *fateor* (line 46)

excellenti animo ac virtute abl. of description

45 **naturae ipsius habitu prope divino** "by the almost superhuman quality of their very nature"

47–48 **naturam sine doctrina . . . sine natura valuisse doctrinam** Note the emphatic CHIASMUS; Cicero touches upon the age-old debate of nature vs. nurture.

48 **quam** Construe with *saepius* (line 47).

valuisse infinitive in indirect discourse

50 **ratio quaedam conformatioque doctrinae** Note HENDIADYS; *quidam* (and its forms) is often used to soften a word choice or expression: "what I might call a systematic program of literary instruction."

50–51 **illud nescio quid praeclarum ac singulare** "some sort of noble and unique excellence"; subject of *solere*, the infinitive in indirect discourse; the idiomatic phrase *nescio quid*, literally "I know not what," serves, in effect, as an indef. pron. ("something").

51–53 [16] **ex hoc esse hunc numero . . . divinum hominem, Africanum** "[I maintain that] in that number/group is . . . this godlike man, Africanus"; the indirect statement introduced by *contendo* (line 49) here continues through line 55; *C. Laelium, L. Furium . . . M. Catonem* (lines 53–55), like *Africanum*, are acc. subjects of the indirect statement.

53 **Africanum** Scipio Africanus the Younger, consul in 147 BCE, conqueror of Carthage in 146, distinguished soldier, statesman, and man of letters

ex hoc sc. *numero*

C. Laelium consul in 140 BCE and intimate friend of Scipio

L. Furium L. Furius Philus, consul in 136 BCE, a leading orator of the day, and a close friend of Scipio; Scipio, Laelius, and Furius were among a coterie of friends and associates, distinguished both for their public service as well as for their devotion to the study of literature, philosophy, and the other noble arts.

54 **fortissimum** probably meant in a moral sense, "most steadfast, stalwart"

55 **M. Catonem** M. Portius Cato, "the Censor" (234–149 BCE), noted for his austerity and high moral character; he was also a man of letters, who wrote treatises (surviving today mostly in fragments) on a wide range of topics (hence *doctissimum*).

qui a connecting rel., "and these men"

56 **nihil** adverbial in force, "not at all"

ad percipiendam "in appreciating"; a gerundive, along with *colendamque*

57 **adiuvarentur** Note the use of the impf. subjunctive in the protasis of this contrary-to-fact condition, emphasizing the continuity of the help these men received from their study of literature.

58 **quod si** "but if"

fructus "profit, gain, advantage"

61–65 The final period of the passage is a simple but powerful statement on the efficacy of literary studies, underscored by the effective use of POLYSYNDETON, juxtaposition of contrasting pairs, and ASYNDETON.

61 **ceterae** sc. *animi remissiones*

61–62 **temporum . . . aetatum . . . locorum** gen. of description or characteristic; construe *omnium* with each of the nouns.

64 **domi** locative

~ *Ad familiares* 14.1

(In the edition by Shackleton-Bailey, **SB 8**)

In the same year in which *Pro Archia* was delivered, P. Clodius Pulcher, a dissolute, unscrupulous, but noble descendant of a patrician family, disgracefully disguised himself as a woman and attended the mysteries of the Bona Dea (rites from which men were excluded). At the ensuing trial for sacrilege, Clodius claimed to have been ninety miles from Rome when the alleged crime was committed; but Cicero had seen him in the city within three hours of the time of his alibi and testified to that effect. Despite his patent guilt, Clodius secured acquittal through bribery and intimidation, an acquittal that subsequently did not escape Cicero's violent condemnation in the Senate. The personal hatred toward Cicero that this provoked in Clodius would ultimately turn into public vindictiveness. In 59 BCE, Clodius, still bent on revenge, arranged to have himself adopted into a plebeian family so that he might run for the office of tribune of the people (an office open only to plebeians). A year later, with the tacit support of the coalition known as the "First Triumvirate" and the consuls of that year, Clodius, now tribune, manipulated the passage of a law that banned from Rome anyone who had put Roman citizens to death without a trial. This bill was obviously aimed retroactively at Cicero, in reference to his actions as consul against the Catilinarian conspirators. Frightened, Cicero panicked; seeing no aid immediately forthcoming, he decided to leave Rome, retiring into exile in northern Greece (March 58 BCE). Shortly after his departure, Clodius secured a formal decree of banishment, barring Cicero from living within four hundred miles of the city. Subsequently, Clodius also managed to have Cicero's house on the Palatine razed and the site consecrated to Liberty; other property owned by Cicero suffered damage and his family was forced to take refuge with relatives.

While Cicero would be recalled (triumphantly) to Rome by action of the Senate less than eighteen months later, the period of his exile was the nadir of his life. Letters to family and friends from that time reveal a sometimes unseemly, but understandable depression on

Cicero's part that led him even to contemplate suicide. This letter, addressed to his wife Terentia, daughter Tullia, and son (Marcus) Cicero in November of 58, underscores the anxieties he feels regarding his decision to leave Rome and the situation in which he finds his family.

1–3 [1] Letters in the Ciceronian corpus generally begin with a heading, noting when and where the letter was written, and containing a traditional salutation. The unabbreviated form of these three lines would read: *Scripta [est epistola] Dyrrhachi ante diem sextum Kalendas Decembris anno 696 [ab urbe condita]* (58). *[M.] TVLLIVS [CICERO] TERENTIAE SVAE, TVLLIOLAE SVAE, CICERONI SVO SALVTEM DICIT.* Thus, the letter was dispatched from Dyrrhachium on November 25, 58.

Roman dates were reckoned backwards (*a.d.* = *ante diem*) from one of three points in the month, the Kalends (*Kalendae*, the first of the month), the Nones (*Nonae*, the fifth), or the Ides (*Idus*, the thirteenth); in March, May, July, and October, however, the Nones and Ides fell on the seventh and fifteenth respectively. The Romans reckoned inclusively, hence in order to convert a Roman date to a modern one, you must subtract the number cited in the Roman date from the modern date of the Nones or Ides and add 1; for a date involving the Kalends, you must subtract the Roman number from the number of days in the month preceding and add 2. Before the Julian reform of the calendar, February had 28 days, March, May, July, and October had 31, and all other months 29. Thus to calculate the above date: 29 – 6 = 23 + 2 = 25 November. The formulaic use of *ante* with the acc. *diem* is peculiar; we would expect rather something like *sexto die ante Kalendas.*

1 **Dyrrhachi** locative; Dyrrhachium, formerly called Epidamnus, an important port in Illyria, where ships coming from Italy (Brundisium) often landed; apparently this letter was initially written in Thessalonica but brought by Cicero to Dyrrhachium, where he dispatched it after adding a postscript (see Appendix A).

2 **Terentiae** Cicero's wife, whom he married *ca.* 80 BCE; they were divorced in 46.

Tulliolae diminutive (indicating affection) of Tullia, the name of Cicero's daughter, who would be about twenty-one years old at the time, and had already been married for more than four years

3 **Ciceroni** i.e., Cicero's son, who was now about seven years old

4 **perfertur ad me** literally, "it is brought to me," i.e., it is reported to me

5 **incredibilem** predicate adj.

6 **me miserum** acc. of exclamation

7–8 **te . . . incidisse** The infinitive, with subject acc., is often used in exclamations: "alas/to think that you have fallen . . ."

7 **ista virtute, fide, probitate, humanitate** abls. of description, referring to Terentia

8–9 **ex quo patre . . . ex eo** = *ex eo patre . . . ex quo*

9 **percipere** another exclamatory infinitive (see line 8), with *Tulliolam* (line 8) as subject

10–11 **cum primum sapere coepit** literally, "from the time when he first began to have discernment"

12 **quae** a connecting rel.; it refers to all those things mentioned in lines 7–11.

facta sc. *esse*; referring back to *quae*

13 **mea culpa** abl. of means

qui subject of *putabam* and *non sequebar* (line 14); its antecedent is implied from the adj. *mea* (i.e., Cicero).

14 **invidebant** Here and in other contemporaneous letters, Cicero claims that his downfall was largely the result of trusting in friends and associates who were jealous of him; he may in particular have had the orator Hortensius in mind.

15 **petebant** Cicero probably has Caesar chiefly in mind, who, despite their differences, had before the exile offered Cicero a position as a *legatus*; Cicero refused that appointment as well as an appointment to Caesar's Agrarian Board.

[2] **quod si** "but if"

nostris consiliis i.e., "my own judgment"; Cicero often uses the pl. when referring to himself (cf. *usi essemus*), a practice common among other Latin authors as well.

16 **sermo** here, closer to "advice"

stultorum i.e., well-meaning friends who gave the wrong advice

18 **dabo operam** *operam dare* + dat., "to work hard at"

mea valetudo Cicero is most likely referring both to his physical and mental health; he realizes that Terentia's considerable troubles need not be exacerbated by worries over his well-being.

19 **tuo labori desit** i.e., undermine your efforts

res possibly referring to the issue of Cicero's health, but more likely to the general circumstances affecting his family as a result of his exile and absence from Rome

quanta . . . quantoque introducing two indirect questions following the main verb *intellego*; *quanto* is abl. of degree of difference with *facilius* (line 20).

20 **manere domi** The implied subject is Cicero.

21 **tr. pl.** = *tribunos plebis*; Cicero refers to the designate or incoming tribunes.

habemus i.e., have them on his side, supporting his return from exile

Lentulum Publius Cornelius Lentulus Spinther, the consul-elect

22–23 **non est desperandum** the impers. use of the gerundive, "we should/must not despair"

24 [3] **familia** Cicero here refers to his household of slaves; realizing that confiscation of his property was imminent, Cicero had given his slaves their freedom subject to certain conditions; he assures Terentia here (as in a previous letter) that she will maintain authority in this matter.

quo modo placuisse scribis amicis faciemus literally, "we (i.e., I) will act in the way in which you write/report has pleased our friends"; i.e., I will do what you tell me our friends think best.

25 **loco** i.e., Thessalonica, where the bulk of this letter was composed, and where Cicero was staying

26 **Plancius** Gnaeus Plancius, quaestor in Macedonia, provided aid and protection to Cicero at this time; a few years later, he was charged with bribery and defended at trial by Cicero.

27–28 **loco magis deserto** i.e., a more secluded location

28 **Piso** L. Calpurnius Piso Caesoninus, consul in 58, was assigned to Macedonia as proconsul; he was hostile to Cicero and his cause.

30 **quem . . . diem** i.e., the day when Cicero might return to Italy; object of *videro*

32 **reciperaro** = *reciperavero*

33 **et vestrae pietatis et meae** Cicero refers both to the dutifulness/loyalty of Terentia and the family toward him and his own toward them (and perhaps toward the country).

34 [4] **Pisonis** C. Calpurnius Piso Frugi (not to be confused with the Piso mentioned above, line 28); the son-in-law of Cicero, quaestor in 58, who worked devotedly on securing Cicero's recall from exile

35 **supra possit** sc. *esse*

ea res i.e., the kindness, courage, and affection of Piso toward the family, mentioned in line 34

ei voluptati double dat.; *gloriae* (line 36) is also dat.

36–37 **de Quinto . . . accusavi** Apparently an argument or some other source of tension had arisen betweenTerentia and Quintus, Cicero's brother.

38 **quam coniunctissimos** modifying *vos*, line 37

39 [5] **egi** sc. *eis gratias*; apparently Terentia had reminded Cicero to send thanks to some friends who had aided her and their cause.

certiorem factum esse *certior fieri* = "to be informed"

40 **quod** object of *scribis*, referring to the entire indirect discourse clause *te vicum vendituram*

vicum property on one of Terentia's estates, perhaps a row of houses

vendituram sc. *esse*

42 **eadem fortuna** i.e., if Cicero's fortunes remain in the same condition as they are currently

44 **tantum** "only this much"

44–45 **erunt in officio** "will do their duty," i.e., remain loyal

45 **efficere** "accomplish our goal," i.e., Cicero's return

46 **tua pecunia** abl. of means

per "by," when used in an entreaty or an oath

47 **puerum perditum perdamus** Note ALLITERATION; Cicero considers his young son already ruined (*perditum*) by the circumstances surrounding his exile; selling off more property that he would someday inherit will only ruin him further.

47–49 **cui si aliquid erit . . . consequatur** i.e., if he has enough to keep him out of need, an average amount of ability and luck will suffice for the rest; antecedent of *cui* (dat. of possession) is *puerum*, i.e., Cicero's son, who is also subject of the verbs *egeat* and *consequatur.*

49 [6] **fac valeas** a common idiom (cf. *cura* [*ut*] *valeas*) meaning simply "be well"

tabellarios "letter carriers"

51 **exspectatio** i.e., the time for waiting, or perhaps the state of suspense

52 **D. a. d. VI K. Decembr. Dyrrhachi** *Data (est epistola) ante diem sextum Kalendas Decembris*; cf. above, line 1.

53 [7] **Dyrrhachium** a short postscript added before sending the letter, the majority of which had been written in Thessalonica before Cicero had departed there; with the names of cities, towns, and small islands, place to which is expressed in the acc.

case without a prep.; note the POLYSYNDETON, or abundance of conjuctions in the first sentence of the postscript (*et . . . et . . . et*), and the ASYNDETON, or lack of connectives in the second sentence.

54 **officiosa** "obliging, courteous"

loci celebritas i.e., the crowdedness of the place

☙ *Pro P. Sestio* 45–46

In 56 BCE, less than a year following his recall from exile, Cicero was able to demonstrate his gratitude to one of those who had worked for his return, the former tribune, Publius Sestius, who was indicted for violence (*de vi*) at the instigation of Clodius (Cicero's arch-enemy). Viewing this indictment as an attack upon himself as well as Sestius, Cicero composed an oration (*Pro P. Sestio*) that sets forth not only a defense of his client and a justification for himself and his actions, but also a stunning manifesto of his political philosophy. As he does in so many of his speeches, the *patronus* Cicero identifies himself with his client to lend weight and authority to his case. His character and actions become the center of attention, overshadowing those of Sestius.

The *Pro Sestio* includes a long narration (sections 6–77), in which Cicero begins to trace Sestius' life and career chronologically, but then suddenly shifts the emphasis to his own character, the characters of his enemies, his exile, and other events of 58–57 BCE. In sections 45–46 of this narrative, Cicero describes why he chose to go into exile rather than to stay and fight it out with Clodius and his henchmen. He likens Clodius' assault upon him to an assault by pirates on a ship (the ship of state as embodied in Cicero), which, along with its passengers, is ultimately saved by Cicero's own self-sacrifice—one on behalf of many (*unus pro omnibus*). The ship-of-state metaphor, prominent in this excerpt, is a recurring and important motif throughout the oration. This selection also offers an excellent example of Latin prose written in the grand style (note, e.g., the apostrophe to the country and to the gods, the elaborate sentence structure, and the copious use of rhetorical devices). In the end, Cicero's speech carried the day, and Sestius was acquitted (cf. Cicero's letter to his brother Quintus, below, pp. 50–53, for Cicero's own analysis of the events).

1 [45] **unum . . . illud** i.e., that one choice, that one option

non nemo an example of the rhetorical device, LITOTES, in which an affirmation is expressed by a negation of its opposite

2 **acris animi magnique** gen. of quality

2–3 **'restitisses . . . oppetisses'** A common tactic of argumentation employed by Cicero in his speeches is to place a possible objection in the mouth of his adversary or another imagined interlocutor, and then proceed to refute it. Here, the *vir fortis* addresses Cicero, using a series of potential subjunctives, indicating what Cicero might/could have done.

3–7 Note the heightened emotional and stylistic level of this sentence, signaled by the emphatic repetition of *te*, the invocation of the *patria, penates,* and *patrii dei*, and the ANAPHORA of *me* (followed by two, stylistically varied prepositional phrases). In the speeches delivered by Cicero directly following his return from exile, he repeatedly asserts that, by retreating into exile without recourse to arms or violence, he saved the state a second time (his first salvific action was thwarting the Catilinarian conspiracy during his consulship; see Introduction). According to this line of thinking, his self-sacrifice preserved the lives of his fellow citizens and the Republic.

4 **testor** "I call you to witness"; the solemn oath, calling upon the fatherland (*patria*), as well as the household (*penates*) and ancestral gods (*patrii dei*), underscores the intensity of Cicero's argument; *testor* introduces an indirect statement, *me . . . dimicationem caedemque fugisse.*

5 **causa** abl. with a preceding gen., "for the sake of"

6 **mea . . . vita** abl. of comparison

7–14 This long, complex sentence is comprised of a contrary-to-fact condition, with two protaseis (conditional clauses), *si . . . accidisset ut* . . . and *si . . . vectores negarent ac . . . mallent,* and an apodosis (conclusion), *iecissem ipse* . . . that introduces a purpose (final) clause (*ut ceteros conservarem . . .*).

7–8 **mihi . . . naviganti** dat., following *accidisset*; note the elegant way in which the datives bracket the two prepositional phrases.

8–10 **ut . . . minitarentur** subjunctive; normal construction following the verb *accido*

9 **praedones** A decade earlier, on the authority of the *Lex Gabinia*, Pompey the Great (Cn. Pompeius Magnus) had been commissioned to rid the Mediterranean of the menace of piracy; while his mission had been largely successful, the threat of marauding pirates remained a real one at this time.

oppressuros sc. *esse*, fut. infinitive in indirect discourse, introduced by *minitarentur* (line 10)

10 **unum** Note emphasis on Cicero's solitary act of salvation; *unus* is repeated in lines 17, 24, and 27.

sibi an indirect reflex., referring to *praedones* (line 9)

dedidissent Subjects of this verb are the *amici*, mentioned in line 8 (they are also identical to the *vectores*, mentioned in the next clause); plpf. subjunctive in a conditional clause introduced by *nisi.*

10–12 **si . . . negarent ac . . . mallent** the second protasis of the contrary-to-fact condition; note the change in tense from plpf. subjunctive (*si . . . accidisset*) to impf. subjunctives.

10 **id** This refers to the ultimatum given by the pirates (in the previous clause) to Cicero's friends and fellow passengers.

11 **interire** complementary infinitive dependent upon *mallent*

quam "than, rather than"; used in conjuction with *mallent* (line 12); construe in this order: *mallent interire quam tradere me hostibus.*

12 **iecissem** plpf. subjunctive, the verb of the apodosis (conclusion) of the contrary-to-fact condition

potius Construe with *quam . . . adducerem* (lines 13–14).

13 **cupidos** with gen. of object (*mei*); here translate "solicitous of," or "attached/partial to."

15–19 [46] **cum . . . cum . . . cum . . .** three subordinating conjs., introducing clauses that describe the circumstances under which Cicero chose to retire into exile; note ANAPHORA here and again with the series of *alii* below.

15 **in hanc rei publicae navem** i.e., the ship of state; construe with *incursurae* (line 18, "ready/poised to attack"), which modifies the subject of the clause, *armatae tot classes* (line 17).

ereptis . . . gubernaculis abl. absolute

senatui dat. of separation rather than the more usual abl.

16 **tempestatibus** "amid storms . . ."

19 **denuntiaretur** sing. verb agreeing in number with closest of three subjects, *direptio*

19–22 **alii . . . alii . . . alii . . . alii . . . alii . . . alii . . .** an extensive catalogue of those who were not supportive of, or even downright hostile to Cicero in his plight

19 **suspicione periculi sui** "owing to a concern over their own danger"

20 **bonorum** the *boni*, "good men, patriots"; those whom Cicero considers to be loyal supporters of the state, especially those who are in agreement with his political viewpoint

25 **depugnarem** deliberative subjunctive, posing a rhetorical question, "was I to fight it out . . . ?"

potius Construe with *quam* (line 26), "rather than."

non dicam intended to qualify and soften the use of the bold word, *exitium*, "ruin, destruction"

26–27 **id quod omnibus impendebat** The phrase is the object of *susciperem ac subirem* (lines 27–28).

27 **unus pro omnibus** the dominant theme of this passage; cf. lines 10, 17, and 24

27–28 **susciperem ac subirem** The ALLITERATION coupled with the powerful rhythm of these final words (in delivery, Cicero most likely elided the final syllable of *susciperem* with the following *ac*) forms an appropriate ending to this emotional passage.

❧ *Ad Quintum fratrem* 2.4 (SB 8)

Publius Sestius, tribune in 57 BCE, worked diligently for Cicero's recall, even to the point of being severely injured by Clodius' thugs in the rioting and street fighting that was a rather common occurrence in the forum that year. In 56, not long after Cicero's return, Sestius was indicted for violence (*de vi*) and successfully defended by Cicero (see above, pp. 46–50). Shortly following the trial, Cicero wrote to his brother Quintus to report the outcome and to share briefly some other domestic news. At the time, Quintus (who was Cicero's junior by about four years), was serving as a legate in Sardinia, under the command of Pompey the Great. Certain allusions in the letter make it clear that, while Cicero certainly felt a debt of gratitude to Sestius, he and Quintus personally considered the tribune ill-tempered and peevish.

1 **Scr.** = *Scripta* [*est epistola*]

3 [1] **a.d. II Id. Mart.** i.e., March 14; on reckoning Roman dates, see above, p. 41.

3–4 **quod . . . rei publicae** The clause explicates and expands upon the the idea contained in the main clause (viz., *omnibus sententiis absolutus est,* line 5, the fact that Sestius was unanimously acquitted), before the main clause is actually stated; *interfuit*, with a gen. of person, indicating "interest" or "importance": translate, "which was extremely important for the Republic."

4–5 **nullam . . . esse** This clause explains the way in which Sestius' unanimous acquittal was of great importance to the state; the subject/acc., verb/infinitive construction is rather loosely employed: the unanimous acquittal of Sestius was important to the state in that it reveals no difference of opinion in such a case.

in eius modi causa "in a case of this sort"

6 **illud quod** anticipates and refers to *hoc* (line 9), the thing that Cicero had accomplished in this trial.

tibi curae . . . esse the double dat. construction

saepe Construe with *intellexeram.*

ne The clause is introduced by the sense inherent in *tibi curae*, i.e., your concern lest I left open an opportunity . . . (*ne . . . relinqueremus . . . locum*, lines 6–7).

cui iniquo "some (personal) enemy"; *cui* = *alicui* following *ne*

7–10 **relinqueremus . . . nos . . . ferremus . . . nos . . . iudicaremur** Here, and throughout the letter, note the use of the first-person pl., where we would expect sing.

8 **illius** i.e., Sestius'

quibusdam in rebus "in certain respects"; take closely with *illius perversitatem.*

9 **ferremus** "bear, put up with"

scito fut. imperative, regularly used with *scio*

hoc object of *consecutos esse*; *ut* introduces a clause that explains the *hoc.*

iudicio "trial"

10 **gratissimi** the superl. opposite of *ingratos*, line 7

10–11 **defendendo moroso homine** gerundive phrase, abl. of means; *moroso*: "peevish, cantankerous"

11 **cumulatissime** "most fully/abundantly"; construe with *satis fecimus.*

ille i.e., Sestius

11–12 **id quod . . . cupiebat** looks ahead to the action in the main clause *Vatinium . . . concidimus* (lines 12–13).

12 **Vatinium** P. Vatinius, tribune in 59, enemy of Sestius and ally of Julius Caesar; Cicero "sliced him to pieces" (*concidimus*, line 13) when examining him as a witness during the trial. Cicero published this interrogation, and it survives today under the name *In Vatinium*; later Cicero and Vatinius reconciled and were on friendly terms.

12–13 **arbitratu nostro** "at my will/pleasure, as I pleased"

13 **dis hominibusque plaudentibus** abl. absolute

14 **Paulus** L. Aemilius Paulus, consul in 50

testis "as a witness"

in Sestium "against Sestius"

15 **nomen Vatini delaturum** sc. *esse*; the *nominis delatio* was the stage of a prosecution in which formal charges were made.

Macer Licinius C. Licinius Macer Calvus, a well-known poet and orator, often mentioned in connection with the circle of the poet Catullus

16 **ab Sesti subselliis** i.e., from the area of benches where Sestius and his supporters were seated; such spectacles were fairly common occurrences in the Roman courts.

17 **defuturum** from *desum* + dat. (here *illi*, referring ironically to Vatinius); sc. *esse*; "fail"

quid quaeris? a common colloquial rhetorical question in Cicero's correspondence, generally used to bring a topic to a close and to introduce a summation

18 **[Vatinius]** considered by editors an unnecessary later addition; cf. [*filius*] below (line 19)

discessit i.e., from the court

19 [2] **[filius]** cf. [*Vatinius*] above (line 18)

20 **Tyrannio** refers to Theophrastus of Amisus, a renowned scholar and teacher, who had come to Rome from Pontus; Tyrannio appears to have been his nickname.

apud me "at my house"; Tyrannio had set up classes in Cicero's house in Rome; Cicero's nephew, young Quintus, was a pupil there.

21 **domus utriusque nostrum** The Cicero brothers were building adjoining houses in Rome.

redemptori here, the building contractor

22 **curavi** sc. *ut solveretur*

contubernalis Cicero cleverly employs this military technical term (which refers to soldiers who share the same tent) in reference to himself and Quintus, whose new homes will be joined under one roof.

23 **fore** = *futuros esse*

tui objective gen. with *amantissima*; note the emphatic placement of the exclamation *me hercule*, which further emphasizes the adj., which is already in the superl. degree.

24 **Crassipede** Furius Crassipes, soon to be the second husband of Tullia; the marriage did not last long.

confecisse "settled things"; Cicero is here referring to the marriage arrangements.

25 **post Latinas** sc. *ferias*; i.e., after the Latin Festival, also called *Latiar*, in honor of Jupiter Latiaris, which was held annually

habentur religiosi "are considered holy days"

ceterum adverbial, "otherwise, in other respects"

26 **erat exiturus** "he (i.e., Crassipes) was about to leave town"; the *sponsalia*, or betrothal ceremony, had to be put off to a later date because it could not take place during these holy days.

De oratore 1.16–20

In the conclusion of his homage to literature and the liberal arts in the *Pro Archia* (see above, pp. 32–39), Cicero asserts that such studies provide a person solace and refuge in difficult times; and indeed, that was certainly the case for him. During two difficult periods in his lifetime, when he was forced to withdraw, more or less, from public life (the first time in the mid-50s BCE, in the wake of a renewed commitment between Pompey, Crassus, and Caesar in the coalition known to history as the "First Triumvirate"; the second time, in the mid-40s, following the victory of Caesar in the Civil War and his subsequent establishment as dictator), Cicero turned to study, reading, and especially writing as a way of channeling his energy and talents, and assuaging his cares. In 55 BCE, he completed *De oratore*, his masterpiece on the art of verbal persuasion. It stands as his finest, most mature, and most original treatise on oratory and rhetoric. Rather than the bland and often boring precepts that were typical of rhetorical handbooks, it is the ideal orator (as the name of the work implies) that stands at the center of the work. A person educated to serve the community in almost any capacity, the ideal orator is the incarnation of wisdom and eloquence (cf. *De inventione* 1.1, above), a true "philosophical orator," or should we say "oratorical philosopher," who is trained in the broadest possible way; an active, universally competent citizen, an ideal that became the model many centuries later for the so-called "Renaissance Man." The work is laid out in three lengthy books and set as a dialogue between a group of famous Roman statesmen and orators from the generation previous to Cicero's, who are on holiday, away from the hustle and bustle of the Roman Forum. This selection comes from the preface to the first book, in which Cicero addresses his brother Quintus, the work's dedicatee, about the scarcity of great orators over the course of time. The reason for such a lack of great speakers, Cicero asserts, is because of the varied and difficult requirements of the art. He then sketches in bold strokes a portrait of his ideal orator that will be developed in great detail throughout the rest of the work.

1 [16] **quibus de causis** an expression meant to summarize the foregoing and introduce the next point; translate "in consideration of these things; considering all this."

2 **miretur** deliberative subjunctive

2–3 **ex omni memoria aetatum, temporum, civitatum** "in the entire history of generations, of ages, and of communities"

4 **hoc** refers to the ability or faculty of speaking effectively.

5–9 **quid . . . quis aliud . . . esse causae putet** another deliberative question; construe these words as the main clause; literally, "what might anyone imagine to be another reason (i.e., for the small number of orators)?" *quis* is not a second interrog., but rather a weak indef. pron.; *causae* is gen., dependent on *quid* . . .

aliud; the dramatic distance between *quid . . . aliud* and *causae* is an example of the rhetorical device called HYPERBATON (Greek for "transposition"), the separation of words that grammatically belong together.

6–8 **in maxima discentium multitudine . . . praemiis** The prep. *in* here carries a concessive force: "in spite of/in view of the enormous number of apprentices (pupils) . . ."

8 **causarum** In this context, the word refers to court cases.

9 **nisi** "except, but"

rei i.e., oratory

9–10 **quandam incredibilem . . . difficultatem** Forms of *quidam*, when placed with an adj., qualify the noun and emphasize its attribute by adding a vagueness to it: "the peculiar and surely incredible scope and difficulty of oratory"; see also below, line 44: *inanem quandam . . . elocutionem*.

10–11 [17] **scientia . . . rerum plurimarum** A broad knowledge of many areas is the fundamental mark of the ideal orator; see below, lines 41–42.

12 **volubilitas** "a ready flow"

conformanda sc. *est*

13–14 **electione . . . constructione verborum** i.e., both choice and arrangement of words

14 **animorum motus** i.e., the emotions; it is essential for the orator to know human emotions, in order to elicit them when and how he wills in the course of his speech; Aristotle called this source of proof *pathos*.

15 **rerum natura** i.e., nature; cf. *De Rerum Natura*, the title of the philosophical poem by Cicero's contemporary, Lucretius

pernoscendi sc. *sunt*; note the ALLITERATION in *penitus pernoscendi*, as well as the redundant emphasis in *penitus* and *per-*.

quod subordinating conj., introducing a causal clause

16 **eorum qui audiunt** i.e., the orator's audience; *eorum* is dependent on *mentibus*; its placement is unusual.

mentibus object of the prep. *in*; note their striking separation (HYPERBATON).

17 **sedandis . . . excitandis** gerundives with *mentibus* (line 16); the whole phrase should be construed in this order: . . . *in aut sedandis aut excitandis mentibus eorum qui audiunt.*

accedat subjunctive, introduced by *oportet* (line 18) and, as usual, without *ut*; translate "to be added, applied."

eodem adv., literally, "to the same point, place"; "likewise"

18–19 Note the extensive use of connectives (POLYSYNDETON) in these lines; the use of POLYSYNDETON here seems to emphasize the long list of requisites that a true orator must possess.

18 **libero** sc. *homine*; literally, "a free man"; we might best translate here as "a gentleman"; the phrase *eruditio libero digna* signifies the learning or culture founded upon the *artes liberales*, arts/study befitting a free person.

19 **subtili** here, "refined, polished"

20–22 [18] **tenenda . . . neque . . . neglegenda est** an elaborate case of CHIASMUS (ABBA order); the ideal orator must also have knowledge of history and law.

21 **exemplorumque vis** "storehouse of examples/precedents"

22–23 **quid . . . plura dicam** an example of PRAETERITIO, the rhetorical device by which a speaker emphasizes something by claiming to pass over it

23 **actione** *Actio* is the normal Ciceronian word for "delivery," one of the five essential "activities of the orator," the others being "invention" (thinking out the material), "arrangement" (ordering it), "style" (putting the ordered material into words), and "memory" (memorizing the speech); the traditional subcategories of delivery were "voice" (*vox*) and "gesture" (*gestus, vultus*), both of which Cicero mentions in this passage.

23–24 Note the amplification of the subject achieved by the ANAPHORA of *quae* (a connecting rel.) in successive clauses; the antecedent of every *quae* is *actione* in the preceding sentence.

25 **quanta sit** indirect question (its subject is *quae*, i.e., *actio*), governed by *declarat* (line 26)

26 **levis** "trivial"; the profession of acting was not considered an honorable option for a Roman citizen; on the other hand, the Romans respected the craft of great actors, and Cicero studied delivery with Roscius, the greatest actor of his day.

cum *cum*-concessive, "although"

oris = *vultus* (gen. sing.)

28 **animo aequo** i.e., without irritation

29 **de thesauro . . . memoria** the fifth activity of the orator (see line 23), which Cicero here calls a universal "treasure-house"

30 **custos** "as a guard"

inventis cogitatisque rebus i.e., those things accomplished by the previous activities of the orator

adhibeatur subjunctive in a subordinate clause in indirect discourse

31 **omnia** i.e., all the qualities of the orator; subject of the indirect statement

32 **peritura** sc. *esse*

[19] **desinamus** hortatory subjunctive (as is *hortemur*, line 34)

33–34 **ex eis rebus . . . constet** "depends on the combination of all these accomplishments"

34 **singulis** Note contrast with *universis* (line 33).

35 **potius** "rather"

36–37 **animo . . . complectantur** "grasp/appreciate fully"; subjunctive (along with *confidant*, line 39) as verb in a jussive noun clause governed by *hortemur* (line 34)

37–38 **neque eis aut praeceptis aut magistris aut exercitationibus** i.e., not by relying on the rules found in rhetorical handbooks, the teachers of the rules, or the exercises designed to implement and practice the rules—the usual sources for those wishing to learn the art of public speaking in Cicero's day; note the POLYSYNDETON.

38 **sed aliis quibusdam** "but by others that are of a different order," i.e., by means of elements that are quite outside the normal routine (as presented in lines 37–38), including an education embracing all the areas Cicero has mentioned previously (*eruditio libero digna*)

39 **se . . . confidant** Construe in this order: *confidant se posse consequi id quod expetunt.*

39–40 [20] **mea . . . sententia** abl.

40 **omni laude cumulatus** "endowed with all praiseworthy qualities"; i.e., the ideal orator

41–42 **omnium rerum . . . scientiam** Cicero reiterates emphatically the point made in lines 10–12 above.

43 **redundet** "acquire fullness"

oportet See line 18 above.

quae connecting rel., whose antecedent is *oratio*; subject of *habet* (line 44)

res here, "subject matter," the substance, the knowledge that must form the basis or foundation for the words, i.e., the speech (*oratio*); the theme of *res* as the foundation for *verba* is one of the central themes of the dialogue; it recalls, perhaps, the justly famous adage of Cato the Elder (234–149 BCE) on composing a speech: *Rem tene, verba sequentur.*

44 **quandam** See above, line 9.

elocutionem here, in a disparaging sense: "verbal exercise, prattle"

Pro T. Annio Milone 24–29

The late 50s BCE were a particularly turbulent period in the Roman state, marked by political strife that often manifested itself in violent demonstrations and actual skirmishes between partisan street gangs. In 53, for example, such disturbances went so far as to disrupt Rome's electoral system; the consuls for that year did not enter office until July (six months late), and subsequent attempts to hold consular elections for the year 52 were frustrated by the political maneuverings of P. Clodius Pulcher, a populist leader and candidate for the praetorship, and T. Annius Milo, who was canvassing for the consulship. The animosity between these two men was long-standing, seeing that Clodius had been the chief instigator of Cicero's exile (58–57 BCE), while Milo, as tribune in 57, had worked with dedication for Cicero's recall. On the 18th of January, 52 BCE, their quarrel came to a violent resolution. Milo had set out from Rome for Lanuvium (a journey of about twenty miles) with a large entourage; he was met (probably by accident) on the Appian Way by Clodius, who was also accompanied by armed attendants. As the parties passed one another, a scuffle broke out and Clodius was killed. His body, taken back to Rome and put on display, was ultimately carried to the senate house, where it was burned, along with the building. To control the further violence that erupted as a result, Pompey was appointed sole consul; he then enacted strict measures to govern future judicial proceedings. Milo was brought to trial in April, on charges of assault and homicide. Cicero, sole counsel for the defense, delivered his speech under novel circumstances, with Pompey sitting as judge, surrounded by an armed guard in the Roman Forum. We are told that Cicero, visibly rattled by the situation, did not speak with his usual effectiveness. Given the animosity that had built up against Milo's case, and the general desire to put a stop to the chain of violence, however, it is unlikely that Cicero's performance at the trial had much effect on the outcome. Milo was convicted and went into exile at Marseilles.

We have evidence that the published version of the *Pro Milone* differs from the speech that Cicero actually delivered, but we do not know for certain the specific changes he made. No matter what deficiencies marked the original oration and its delivery, critics today agree that the speech as transmitted to us stands as a rhetorical masterpiece. The passage excerpted here comprises the *narratio* (or statement of facts) of that speech. One of the traditional parts of an oration, the narration's purpose was to state in a brief, clear, and persuasive manner the facts of the case (at least the version of the facts as perceived or portrayed by the speaker and his client). Here Cicero lays the groundwork for making the argument that it was Clodius who set the ambush for Milo, and not vice versa. The clarity and lucidity of this simple narrative have been justly praised by students of Cicero throughout the ages.

1–10 [24] Cicero begins his *narratio* with a lengthy period that sets out the circumstances under which Clodius acted. *P. Clodius*, the subject of the sentence (placed emphatically at the beginning of the section) is finally followed by the main verbs, *reliquit* and *transtulit*, in line 7.

1 **omni scelere** abl. of means

in praetura Clodius was a candidate for the office of praetor

2 **tracta esse** infinitive in indirect discourse; "had been delayed"

anno superiore "in the previous year"

3 **non multos mensis** The normal length of a term of office in Rome was one year; because the elections had been delayed and the chief magistrates for 53 BCE did not assume office until July (see introduction above), they ended up serving less than six months.

3–4 **qui . . . spectaret** antecedent is Clodius; unlike the others (*ceteri*), he did not respect the instrinsic merit of the office of praetor.

4 **ut** "as"

5 **vellet** the second of two verbs in the *qui*-clause

conlegam i.e., "*as* a colleague"

effugere "avoid"; Clodius wanted to avoid serving in office with an upright and scrupulous colleague (L. Paulus); all of Cicero's language is aimed at painting Clodius' character in an unfavorable manner.

7 **annum suum** "his proper/regular year"; Roman law (the *Lex Villia*) specified the earliest age and the proper intervals at which political offices could be held; Clodius had served as aedile in 56 and could have stood for praetor in 54 (to serve in 53, the year in which the terms of office had been cut short); it was

generally considered an honorable (and desirable) accomplishment for a man to gain political office in the first year in which he was eligible; Cicero, in another context, boasts that he was elected to all of his public offices *anno suo.*

7–8 **ut fit, religione aliqua** "because of some religious scruple, as commonly happens"; e.g., the occurrence or announcement of some unfavorable omen

8 **quod** Here, translate "as."

8–9 **ad . . . gerendam . . . ad evertendam** *ad* + gerundives to indicate purpose

9 **hoc est** "or rather" or "that is to say . . ."

10 **plenum annum atque integrum** object of *haberet* (line 8)

[25] **occurrebat ei** as in our expression, "it occurred to him. . ."; i.e., he realized

mancam "crippled"

11 **futurum** sc. *esse*

consule Milone abl. absolute

eum i.e., Milo; Clodius is the subject of *videbat* (line 12).

12 **fieri** "was bound to be, was sure to be, was being voted for"

13 **contulit se** "he attached himself, he went over to"

eius i.e., Milo's

ita "in such a way, on condition that . . ."; introduces a result clause

14 **petitionem** "campaign, canvass"

etiam invitis illis abl. absolute; *illis* refers to Milo's competitors/fellow candidates.

15 **dictitabat** a "frequentative" form of the verb; "he kept reiterating"

15–18 Note Cicero's effective use of the impf. tense in these lines to describe vividly ongoing action in past time.

16 **tribus** acc. pl.

se interponebat "acted as a go-between"; perhaps "offered himself as a (bribery) agent"

Collinam novam "a new Colline tribe"; the four city tribes, populated largely by the poor and freedmen, were ranked lowest of the thirty-five tribes and voted last in order; the Colline was considered the least reputable of the city tribes; Cicero is not speaking literally (that Clodius actually registered a new Colline tribe), but wants to convey the notion that Clodius recruited a host of unsavory, unscrupulous characters and distributed them among the tribes.

17–18 **quanto . . . tanto** abls. of degree of difference, used correlatively with compars.; "the more . . . the more . . ."

17 **ille** i.e., Clodius; *hic* (line 18) refers to Milo.

miscebat *Misceo* often carries the connotation of "stirring up trouble or confusion"; cf. the common idiom, *omnia miscere*, "to cause general confusion."

18 **in dies** "day by day, daily"

homo i.e., Clodius

18–19 **ad omne facinus paratissimus** describes *homo* (line 18).

19 **virum** i.e., Milo

20–22 **idque . . . declaratum** almost a parenthetical remark, explicating the assertion that Milo was considered *certissimum consulem* (i.e., "quite certain to become consul"); *id* refers to that point; subject of *intellexit* is Clodius.

21 **suffragiis** Because there had been a number of failed attempts to complete elections, the votes of many of the tribes had already been made known.

22 **occidendum** sc. *esse*

23 [26] **agrestis** "savage, crude"

quibus We would normally expect abl. of agent, *a quibus*.

23–24 **silvas publicas . . . Etruriamque** government-owned land was often rented out for use as pastures and as a resource for the harvesting of timber; Clodius had extensive land holdings in Etruria; Cicero asserts that Clodius had exploited such properties or harassed those who had paid rent to the state for their use.

24–25 **depopulatus erat** (verb in *quibus* clause)

vexarat . . . deduxerat subject of these verbs is Clodius

25 **minime obscura** i.e., "patently clear"; affirming something by denying its opposite is the use of the rhetorical device known as LITOTES.

26 **Miloni** dat. of separation with *eripi*

27 **significavit** "he intimated, hinted at"

28 **quin etiam** "even more"

M. Favonio Marcus Favonius, a staunch opponent of Clodius, a friend of Cato the Younger (line 31), and later one of the assassins of Julius Caesar

29 **eo** i.e., Clodius

qua spe fureret indirect question introduced by the pple. *quaerenti* (line 28); subject of *fureret* is Clodius.

Milone vivo abl. absolute

illum i.e., Milo

30 **summum** here, an adv., "at most"

vocem "remark"

31 **M. Catonem** Marcus Porcius Cato Uticensis, sometimes called "the Younger" (95–46 BCE), was the great grandson of Cato the Censor, the Elder. Committed to Stoic principles, opponent of Clodius, he was known for his constancy and uprightness (some would say, obstinancy). He committed suicide in 46 rather than accept a pardon from Caesar.

[27] **cum** "since"

32 **Lanuvinis** the inhabitants of Lanuvium (below, lines 34–35)

33 **sollemne** "yearly, annual," especially when referring to religious rites or ceremonies

legitimum "established by law"

33–34 **ante diem XIII Kalendas Februarias** i.e., January 18; in the pre-Julian calendar, January had only twenty-nine days.

34 **Miloni** dat. of possession, with *esse* in indirect discourse

Lanuvium With names of cities, towns, and small islands, Latin expresses place to which by the acc. case without a prep.

35 **dictator** here, merely the chief magistrate of the town; Milo hailed from Lanuvium, a town located in Latium about twenty miles southeast of Rome; as its current *dictator*, it was obligatory for him to journey there for the formal declaration/inauguration of the priest of Juno Sospita (*ad flaminem prodendum*), whose famous temple was located there.

Lanuvi locative

Roma abl., expressing place from which

36 **ipse** i.e., Clodius

fundum "estate, homestead"

36–37 **quod re intellectum est** a parenthetical remark: "as has been ascertained/made clear by what happened"

38 **ut** introducing a clause of result

39 **quae . . . quam** Both rel. prons. have their antecedent in *contionem* (line 38).

nisi introducing a contrary-to-fact condition in past time

39–40 **obire facinoris locum tempusque** literally, "to go to meet the time and place of his deed"; i.e., to be present in a timely way at the scene of his crime

41 [28] **quoad** The Senate adjourned that day between 10:00 and 11:00 a.m. (the fourth hour).

43 **dum se uxor, ut fit, comparat** With a generalization about wives' behavior, Cicero surely hopes to amuse and ingratiate himself with the predominantly male audience.

44 **id temporis** "at that point in time"

44–45 **cum . . . potuisset** Cicero's point here is that Clodius, if he were not purposely delaying in order to ambush Milo, could have already (*iam*, line 44) returned to Rome by that time.

45 **obviam fit** followed by the dat. (cf. line 51); the encounter occurred near Bovillae, a small town about nine miles from Rome.

46 **expeditus** "unencumbered," i.e., ready for action; the following contrasting portraits of Clodius and Milo are aimed at establishing an argument based on probability, that it was Clodius who intended to ambush Milo, and not vice versa; Cicero avoids consideration of what may have been the actual truth of the matter, i.e., that the encounter was merely coincidental.

raeda a four-wheeled traveling carriage; Milo is traveling by *raeda* (line 49, below), hardly a vehicle from which one would plan and launch an attack, while Clodius is on horseback.

46–47 Note the emphatic ANAPHORA of *nulla . . . nullis . . . nullis.*

47 **Graecis comitibus, ut solebat** Apparently it was Clodius' custom of traveling with a large retinue of companions that would have included (Greek) musicians and entertainers.

48 **quod numquam fere** sc. *fecit*

hic insidiator i.e., Milo; Cicero speaks ironically, of course; *hic* here means something like "this so-called."

ad with gerundive to indicate purpose

50 **paenulatus** i.e., wearing the *paenula*, a heavy traveling cloak, something like a poncho (hence, constricting easy arm movement); in contrast to Clodius, who is *expeditus* (line 46, above)

50–51 **magno . . . comitatu** Cicero uses four adjs. to characterize the retinue accompanying Milo and his wife, emphasizing again its unsuitability for launching an ambush; that young boys and girls were present most likely indicates that they were intended to participate (perhaps by singing or dancing) in the ceremony to be held in the temple of Juno Sospita (see above, line 35). Note the intentional accumulation of connectives, i.e., POLYSYNDETON (*et . . . et . . . ac*), contrasting in tempo vividly with the ASYNDETON and ANAPHORA of *nulla* and *nullis* in lines 46–47, describing Clodius.

50 **impedito** precisely the verbal opposite of the word (*expeditus*) used of Clodius in line 46, above

52 **hora fere undecima** i.e., about 4:30–5:00 p.m.

53–66 Throughout this section, Cicero employs language appropriate for describing battles and other military encounters.

53 **hunc** i.e., Milo

de loco superiore "from higher ground," i.e., from a strategically advantageous position

54 **adversi** "opposite, against," in a hostile sense; i.e., confronting (attacking/obstructing) the carriage, they kill the driver

hic i.e., Milo

55 **reiecta paenula** abl. absolute

56–57 **partim . . . partim** here "some . . . others"

57 **a tergo** "from behind, from the rear"

58 **quod** "because"

hunc i.e., Milo

59 **eius servos** i.e., Milo's slaves

post adverbial

quibus Antecedent is *servos.*

59–60 **animo fideli . . . praesenti** abl. of description or characteristic; *praesenti,* i.e., "ready"; cf. our saying, "presence of mind"

61 **cum** subordinating conj. governing four verbs in impf. subjunctive, all describing the circumstances under which the main action occurred

pugnari impers. use of the pass. infinitive: "there was fighting/a fight was going on"

62 **occisum** sc. *esse*

et . . . et "both . . . and"

ex "from"

63 **re vera** "really, truly"

64 **derivandi criminis** "shifting/diverting the charge"

causa with a preceding gen.

ut factum est "just as it happened"

64–65 **nec imperante . . . domino** abl. absolute

65 **quod** Antecedent is *id*, line 63.

65–66 **quod . . . voluisset** a euphemistic way of saying that Milo's slaves killed Clodius to avenge their master's (supposed) murder

Ad familiares 16.4 (SB 123)

In March of 51 BCE, Cicero, as an ex-consul who had not held a governorship abroad, was assigned the province of Cilicia. Although he was not at all enthusiastic about assuming this assignment, he governed the province well during this year and even garnered for himself a *supplicatio* from the Senate for his military actions against one of the warring local tribes. Relieved of his duties on July 30, 50 BCE, he set out leisurely for Rome, accompanied by his brother, his nephew, his son, and his freedman Marcus Tullius Tiro, who took ill at Patrae (modern Patras) and was forced to remain there until he recovered sufficiently to travel.

Tiro had been freed by Cicero in 53 (hence his full name, taken from his former master). He had been well educated from boyhood and served for years as Cicero's personal secretary and even as his literary advisor. Tiro himself was an active editor and author; he published some of Cicero's letters and speeches after Cicero's death, and wrote several books about his former master, including one on Cicero's wit and humor. He reputedly lived to be almost one hundred. This letter, like the others in the collection that are addressed to Tiro, displays vividly the great regard in which Cicero held Tiro, indeed as a virtual family member.

1 **Scr.** = *Scripta [est epistola]*

Leucade Leucas, an island off the coast of western Greece, in the Ionian Sea (see Appendix A)

VII Id. Nov. a. 704 = *ante diem* VII *Idus Novembris anno 704 [ab urbe condita]*; November 7, 50 BCE; for the method of calculating Roman dates, see above, p. 41.

2 **S. P. D.** = *salutem plurimam dicit*

3 **Q. F.** = *Quinti filius*; i.e., Cicero's nephew, the son of Cicero's brother, Quintus

4 [1] **varie** i.e., with varying emotions

5 **altera** sc. *pagina*

5–7 **non dubito quin . . . committas** A subjunctive clause with *quin* is the normal expression with *non dubito* ("I do not doubt").

6 **quoad** "until"

7 **satis . . . mature** "soon enough"

8 **confirmatum** sc. *te*

bene existimari probably impers. passive; "is well thought of, has a good reputation"

10 **ius** "broth, soup"

quom an old form of *cum*

κακοστόμαχος literally, "bad stomach"; "having a sensitive stomach"

12 **Lysonem** Tiro was staying at the house of Lyso, Cicero's host at Patrae.

[2] **Curium** Manius Curius, a Roman businessman living in Patrae, and a friend to Atticus and Cicero

13 **summi offici summaeque humanitatis** gen. of description

in his i.e., in Cicero's communications with Curius

14 **videretur** i.e., "seems best"

ad se i.e., to his house

traferret = *transferret*; the *ut*-clause is an indirect command (jussive noun clause), introduced by the sense of commanding implied in *scripsi* (line 13; cf. lines 19–20).

14–15 **Lyso . . . noster** subject of the verb in the fear-clause, *vereor ne . . . sit* (line 15); the placement before its clause is emphatic.

15–16 **quia omnes Graeci** sc. *sunt*; the comment illustrates a typical Roman attitude toward the Greeks.

17–18 **quid faciendum sit** passive periphrastic in an indirect question, introduced by *iudicabis*

18 **illud** Construe with *quod*, line 19.

sumptu contracted form of the dat. (*sumptui*), following *parcas* (line 19)

20 **quod dixisses daret** sc. *ut* and construe in this order: *ut daret quod dixisses.*

medico ipsi indirect object

aliquid i.e., monetary compensation

21 **quo** = *ut eo*; generally used in purpose (final) clauses that contain a compar. (*studiosior*)

21–24 [3] Cicero lists all the areas in which Tiro's services have been crucial to him.

24 **viceris** "you will top them all"; notice the use of the fut. pf. tense (cf. *videro*) in this condition.

25 **si recte erit** i.e., if things go well

cum quaestore Mescinio Lucius Mescinius Rufus, who had served as Cicero's quaestor while in Cilicia

decursurum sc. *esse*; "run down"; here "sail down," i.e., from Patrae to Leucas

27 **valetudini tuae** dat., following *consulueris*

28 **consulito** fut. imperative

29 [4] **nihil laboro, nisi ut** a rather indirect way of saying, "My sole concern is that . . ."

sic habeto another fut. imperative; "understand/know this"

30 **qui me amet** rel. clause of characteristic, following a negative antecedent (*neminem*)

quin "who . . . not"

idem subject of phrase *te amet*; English would normally here use an adv., "likewise."

30–31 **cum . . . tum** "both . . . and"

31 **interest** the impers. use of *intersum*, meaning "it is of importance, it is of concern"; the construction is idiomatic and somewhat complicated: the person (or thing) concerned is placed in

the feminine abl. (or sometimes gen.) of the possessive pron. (cf. *tua et mea*); the cause of concern is expressed by the infinitive or acc. with infinitive (cf. *te valere*).

multis . . . curae double dat.

32 **adhuc** "up to this time," i.e., in the past; contrasted with *nunc* (line 33)

nullo loco = *nulla in re*

te confirmare i.e., recover your strength

35 **tanti . . . fieri** *Fio* when used with a gen. of price or value means "to be valued"; *tanti* (gen.) is correlative with *quantam* (line 34); *me* is the subject of the indirect statement (*tanti me fieri*) introduced by *iudicabo*; *a te* is abl. of agent.

36 **Lepta** Quintus Paconius Lepta, who served as Cicero's *praefectus fabrum* ("chief engineer," generally functioning as adjutant to the commander) in Cilicia

37 **VII Id. Nov. Leucade** see above, line 1

Ad familiares 14.18 (SB 144)

When Cicero, having finished his tour of duty in Cilicia, finally reached Rome, he found the political situation in turmoil and the state on the brink of civil war. Following the death of Crassus in Parthia a few years earlier, the unofficial alliance of Crassus, Pompey, and Caesar (i.e., the so-called "First Triumvirate") had crumbled; and from that time the relationship between Pompey and Caesar had been deteriorating increasingly. News that Caesar had crossed the Rubicon on January 10, accompanied by his armed legions, threw panic into those in Rome. Pompey moved south on January 17, and was followed by the consuls and other prominent citizens, including Cicero (who left for Formiae). Pompey had asked him to supervise the coastal areas south of Rome. When Cicero set out, he took his son with him, but left his wife and daughter in Rome. In this letter, written a few days later, he debates over what would be the best course of action for them.

1 **Scr.** = *Scripta* [*est epistola*]

Formiis locative; Formiae, a coastal city in southern Latium, where Cicero owned a villa

IX K. Febr. a. 705 = *ante diem* IX *Kalendas Februarias anno 705* [*ab urbe condita*]; January 22, 49 BCE; for the method of calculating Roman dates, see above, p. 41.

3 **Cicero** i.e., Marcus, Cicero's son

S. D. P. = *salutem dicunt plurimam*

4 [1] **considerandum** sc. *esse*; pass. periphrastic, introduced by *puto* (line 5), with dat. of agent (*vobis*)

5 **quid faciatis** indirect question, dependent on *considerandum* (line 4)

-ne . . . an . . . an three alternatives as possible answers to the indirect question, *quid faciatis*

6 **consilium** here, close to "decision"

7 **mihi veniunt in mentem** "come to mind, occur to me"

8 **tuto** here an adv.; Cicero could have written *tutas* instead.

Dolabellam P. Cornelius Dolabella; previously defended by Cicero in two court cases, he married Cicero's daughter Terentia in 50; if Tullia and Terentia remained in Rome, they could avail themselves of his protection, seeing that he was now a supporter of Caesar.

8–9 **nobis adiumento esse** double dat.; the "help" that Cicero mentions probably is in reference to his property holdings in Rome.

9 **si quae** = *si aliquae*

10 **quod** introduces a clause that explains *illud*.

bonos i.e., patriots, those who support the cause of the Republic and Pompey

11 **Roma** abl.

12 **regio** i.e., Campania, a region south of Latium where Cicero had towns friendly to him under his patronage, as well as privately held estates (*oppidorum . . . praediorum*, lines 12–13; the gens. are descriptive of *regio*)

12–13 **cum . . . tum** "both . . . and"

14 **commode . . . esse** i.e., to live comfortably

in nostris i.e., in estates or properties owned by Cicero

15 [2] **constat** impers., "it is clear"

utrum i.e., whether to remain or leave Rome

16 **isto loco** "in your position/station"

ne The clause takes its force from the meaning implicit in *videte* (line 15): "watch out/look out/see to it lest . . ."

17 **velim** with a subjunctive (here *consideretis*, line 18) or infinitive, the equivalent to an optative subjunctive (i.e., a subjunctive expressing a wish): "I should like to have you consider"; see lines 19–20 for the same construction.

19 **Philotimo** Philotimus, Terentia's freedman, who often assisted Cicero with financial and domestic affairs; dat. following *dicetis*

dicetis fut. indicative used for the imperative; here its position follows the jussive noun clause in lines 18–19 (to be construed in this order: *ut domus habeat propugnacula et praesidium)*, which is dependent on it.

20 **certos** "sure, reliable"

22 **VIIII K. Formiis** see above, line 1; note the alternate way of writing the Roman numeral IX.

Ad familiares 14.20 (SB 173)

Ad familiares 14.20 is the last extant letter from Cicero to his wife, Terentia. Its tone stands in stark contrast with that of the previous letter (see above, pp. 70–72). It seems that during the year 48, the couple became increasingly estranged from one another, perhaps stemming from some suspicions Cicero harbored concerning Terentia's handling of their financial affairs while he was away from Rome during the Civil War. Cicero had met Caesar a few days earlier at Brundisium and secured from him permission to remain in Italy; he now sets out for his Tusculan villa and curtly and coldly instructs his wife on preparing the house for his arrival. Cicero and Terentia were divorced a few months later.

1 **Scr.** = *Scripta* [*est epistola*]

Venusino i.e., in the area near Venusia, a town in southern Italy, north of Brundisium on the Appian Way

K. Oct. a. 707 = *Kalendis Octobribus anno 707* [*ab urbe condita*]; October 1, 47 BCE; for the method of calculating Roman dates, see above, p. 41.

2 **S. D.** = *salutem dicit*

3 **venturos** sc. *esse*

Nonis "on the Nones"; in October, the Nones were on the seventh day of the month.

4 **ut sint omnia parata** a command for which some introductory phrase (e.g., "see to it that . . . ," "make sure that . . .") must be supplied

6 **ut sit** for this type of command, see above (line 4).

7 **ad victum** literally, "for living"; i.e., for support, nourishment, subsistence

7–8 **K. Oct. de Venusio** see above (line 1)

~ *Brutus* 1–9

Brutus, subtitled *De claris oratoribus*, is another of Cicero's important rhetorical works; in it he traces the history and development of oratory in Rome. Cicero composed *Brutus* probably in early 46 BCE, fashioning it as a dialogue between Brutus (the dedicatee, and, on the Ides of March, two years later, one of Caesar's assassins), Atticus (Cicero's closest friend and confidant), and Cicero himself, as they wait for news about Caesar's war in Africa (one of the final campaigns of the Civil War).

In this passage, which constitutes the preface of the dialogue, Cicero eulogizes the great orator Hortensius, his rival and friend, who had died a few years earlier; Hortensius' character serves as a symbol of free eloquence in a free state. This mournful tribute sets the tone for Cicero's deeper and broader lament over the demise of oratory and the Republic in general, a lament whose tone colors the dialogue throughout. Cicero uses the occasion to comment as well on his own career at this difficult time. *Brutus* is a work of both history and literary criticism. It is also a work of great stylistic beauty, as this preface amply illustrates.

1 [1] **Cilicia** Roman province located in southern Asia Minor (modern southwestern Turkey); Cicero served as proconsul there from July 51 to August 50 BCE, during which time he distinguished himself as an upright and just governor and an able military commander.

decedens the technical term for a governor leaving his province

Rhodum Rhodes, an island off the southwestern coast of Asia Minor; as a young man, Cicero had studied oratory there.

eo locative: "there"

2 **Q. Hortensi** Quintus Hortensius Hortalus (114–50 BCE, consul in 69) was the foremost orator in Rome before Cicero's arrival on the scene; as a young pleader, Cicero faced him as an opponent in several important cases (e.g., the trial of Verres), but later collaborated with him on many defenses; Hortensius ultimately sponsored Cicero in the office of augur (see below).

opinione abl. (of comparison) by virtue of the force of *maiorem* (line 3); the opinion or assumption of the casual observer (*omnium*) would be that the rivalry between the two orators was a source of friction rather than friendship.

3–6 **nam . . . dolebam** a rather complicated but beautifully constructed period, containing a compound sentence, each verb of which (*videbam, dolebam*) is introduced by *et*, each in turn introducing an indirect statement (*me privatum* [*esse*], *dignitatem . . . deminutam* [*esse*])

3–4 **cum . . . tum** "both . . . and"; linking two abls. of separation, each dependent on *privatum* (line 5)

5 **auguris** "augur," a member of the Priestly College of Augurs, official Roman diviners who advised the Senate and magistrates concerning signs indicating the will of the gods; their election was referred to as *cooptatio*, a choice, at this date based on the nomination by two current members and ratified by popular vote; membership, highly regarded as a reward for distinguished public service, was for life; as we learn below (lines 7–9), Hortensius nominated Cicero for this honor.

dignitatem "prestige"

6 **conlegi** here, "college" (i.e., the College of Augurs)

7–8 **et cooptatum . . . et inauguratum** pf. pass. infinitives (sc. *esse*) in indirect discourse, both introduced by *recordabar* (line 7); for the meaning of *cooptatum*, see note on *auguris*, line 5 above.

8 **iudicium dignitatis meae** The nominator made a solemn declaration of his candidate's worthiness for the office.

inauguratum "installed," i.e., formally inducted into the College of Augurs

9 **ab eodem** i.e., Hortensius

ex quo "on the basis of which, so that"

in parentis . . . loco This Latin phrase is still used today, usually in reference to the responsibilities that schools and teachers exercise in relation to their students; for a Roman of Cicero's time, it undoubtedly recalled the strong familial relationships between children and their father (*paterfamilias*), as well as magistrates and their superiors.

eum notice the dramatic placement of the word within the prepositional phrase; such a violation of expected word order is called HYPERBATON.

10 **colere** here, "to pay constant attention to, to cultivate the friendship of, to devote oneself to"

[2] **molestiam** "burden, troublesomeness, chagrin"

quod The clause introduced by *quod* (= "the fact that") serves as the subject of the verb *augebat.*

10–11 **magna . . . penuria** abl., describing the circumstances or situation at the time of Hortensius' passing

12 **consiliorum omnium societate** Construe with *coniunctissimus* (line 11).

13 **alienissimo** modifying *tempore*: "most inopportune"; at the time, Rome was on the brink of civil war.

14 **desiderium** "longing, regret for"

dolebamque the second impf. verb in this long period, parallel to *augebat* (line 10)

15 **non** Construe with *adversarium.*

ut plerique putabant For the thought, see above, lines 2–3.

15–17 **adversarium . . . amiseram** Note the pleasing balance and parallelism of this clause.

17 **gloriosi laboris** Cicero refers to their collaboration in many court cases and their work as public officials on behalf of the state.

17–18 [3] **leviorum artium** "less important arts," e.g., poetry, music, grammar; these were considered by Cicero to be inferior or less important than the arts of oratory and statesmanship.

18 **memoriae proditum est** "it has been recorded, committed to writing"

nobilis = *nobiles*

19 **aequalium** i.e., peers, contemporaries

quo . . . animo "with what sort of spirit/feeling"; interrog. phrase introducing a rhetorical question

20 **certare** The infinitive here (as well as the parallel infinitive *habere*, line 21) acts as subject of the verb *erat.*

quam "than"; with the compar. adj. *gloriosius*

21 **cum** introducing a causal clause, continuing the thought of the previous sentence

21-23 **non modo . . . sed contra** a variation of *non solum . . . sed etiam*; thus *contra* is here adverbial.

22 **illius** i.e., of Hortensius; construe with *cursus.*

cursus "career"; perhaps even referring more specifically to the *cursus honorum*, or course of public offices pursued by those interested in election to the magistracies of the state

23-24 **et communicando et monendo et favendo** Note the slow, sonorous, and emphatic ending of this period achieved by the use of many connectives (POLYSYNDETON) and the series of gerunds in the abl. case.

25 [4] **usus** pf. pple. of *utor* + abl.; "having enjoyed"

suo contrasted (in line 26) with *suorum civium tempore*

26 **tum . . . cum** "at a time when"

27 **rem publicam** object of both *lugere* and *iuvare*

28 **tam diu quam** "as long as"

in civitate i.e., in a free state

29 **nostro incommodo detrimento** Construe closely with *doleamus.*

30 **vero** "but"; marking a strong contrast with the previous clause

opportunitatem "fit time, timely occasion"

benevolentia Here the word seems to imply the happiness that one experiences over the good fortune of a friend.

31 **prosequamur** "attend/accompany (with honor)"; hortatory subjunctive (as is *doleamus*, line 29)

33-34 [5] **quod . . . licet** The clause constitutes an explication and expansion of *id* (line 33)

34 **eo** "him," i.e., Hortensius; abl. case with *frui*

35 **domesticam** "personal"

36 **tamquam** for *tamquam si*, "just as if"; governing the subjunctive verb *acciderit* (line 37)

acerbitatis partitive gen.; note the ALLITERATION/ASSONANCE of the *a*-sound at the beginning of this and the next three words.

38 **satis** qualifying *grato*

39–41 [6] **si viveret . . . desideraret . . . sustineret** a contrary-to-fact, pres. condition

40 **una cum . . .** "along/together with"

bonis literally the "good" citizens; in Cicero's view, those patriotic citizens who stood for the same political principles that he embraced

hunc modifies *dolorem* in line 41; note how the adj. and noun literally embrace the two qualifying prepositional phrases, introduced by *praeter* and *cum* respectively.

41 **ceteros** sc. *cives*

42 **fuisset** Subjunctive by attraction regularly occurs with subordinate verbs in indirect discourse.

quasi "as it were"; used to soften the metaphor in *theatrum*

43 **voce** abl. of separation following the verbs of the indirect statement, *spoliatum atque orbatum* (*esse*); modified by the adjs. *erudita* and *digna* (lines 43–44)

Romanis Graecisque auribus abl., following *digna* (line 44); while Cicero mourns the death of Hortensius in this passage, he is also actually lamenting what he considers to be the death (or at least near-death) of the Republic as he knows it, illustrated by curtailed or restricted opportunities for speaking in the courts, the assembly, and the Senate, as a result of Caesar's dictatorship.

44–45 [7] **equidem angor animo** *Equidem* is used by Cicero only with the first person sing. form of the verb; Cicero now shifts the focus from Hortensius to his own situation; at the point in his life and career at which his talents and authority as an orator and a statesman should be most highly regarded, the situation brought on by the Civil War and its aftermath has wreaked havoc with such expectations.

45 **non . . . armis** Note the emphasis and intensification of this phrase, containing the ANAPHORA of *non* with three gens. dependent on *armis* (a good example of what is often called an "ascending tricolon"); these sorts of *arma* are set in stark contrast to the *arma* mentioned below in line 49.

45–46 **armis egere rem publicam** indirect statement introduced by *angor* (line 44); *egere* (here meaning "desire, need") governs the abl. (*armis*).

46–47 **quae . . . quibusque . . . quaeque** Antecedent for each is *armis* (line 45).

47 **propria** "proper, peculiar"

47–48 **cum . . . tum** "both . . . and"

48 **bene moratae . . . civitatis** i.e., a highly principled, civilized state in possession of a sound constitution

48–49 **quod si** "but if"

50–51 **auctoritas et oratio** These, of course, are the sorts of weapons that statesmen like Hortensius and Cicero were capable of wielding.

51 **tum profecto fuit cum** "it was precisely then when . . ."

patrocinium This word is used to denote the services that a patron or advocate provides to his client; hence, "defense, protection"

52 [8] **nobismet ipsis** Often Cicero uses the pl. to refer to his own personal situation; this long and complicated period begins with the introduction of a noun clause (*accidit ut . . . doleremus*), interrupted by a concessive clause (*quamquam . . .*); two temporal clauses (*quo tempore . . .* , line 54, and *cumque . . .* , line 57) are then inserted before the resumption of the *quod* clause (*tum arma . . .*) begun in line 54; ending finally with a rel. clause (*quibus illi ipsi*, line 59) that introduces another rel. clause (*qui didicerant . . .* , line 59) and an indirect question (*quem ad modum . . .* , line 60).

53 **multo** abl. of degree of difference with *magis*

54 **aetas** Here the word carries the connotation of a lifetime of work and accomplishment; a career.

55 **tamquam** designed to soften the metaphor inherent in *in portum*; i.e., Cicero (like a ship heading for harbor) was hoping in his senior years to find a haven of moderate and honorable leisure; in other contexts, he speaks of *otium cum dignitate.*

56 **deberet** "had the right"

57 **canesceret** The metaphor is taken from a mature person whose hair has begun to turn gray.

58 **quandam** Forms of *quidam*, when placed with an adj., qualify the noun and emphasize its attribute by adding a vagueness to it.

quasi "as it were/so to speak"; inserted again to soften the metaphor and the application of a term normally associated with people (i.e., *senectutem*) to oratory or oratorical style (*oratio*, line 57)

59 **quibus** Antecedent is *arma*; in the abl. case by virtue of the verbs *uti* and *uterentur* (line 60) in the subsequent clauses

illi ipsi, qui . . . i.e., Pompey and Caesar, the chief protagonists of the Civil War

60 **quem ad modum** "how"; acting as a subordinating conj. of an indirect question introduced by *reperiebant* (line 61)

62–63 [9] **cum . . . tum** This appearance of this combination twice in two successive lines, "both . . . and," is somewhat unusual.

63 **quibus** Antecedent is *ei* (line 61); dat. with *licuit*, line 64.

rerumque gestarum i.e., *res gestae*, "accomplishments"

64 **quorum** transitional rel., referring to *quibus . . . perfrui licuit* (lines 63–64)

memoria et recordatio i.e., both the memory and the act of recalling it

65 **sane** modifying *iucunda*, emphasizing the pleasantness of the recollection in stark constrast with *maximis . . . gravissimisque curis*

66 **in eam** i.e., into the act of recollection

ex "as the result of"; with this line, the preface concludes; after a brief description of the physical surroundings, the dialogue between Cicero, Brutus, and Atticus begins in earnest.

De amicitia 19–23

Following Caesar's victory in the Civil War and his subsequent establishment as dictator, Cicero took little part in politics. The grief that he felt over the condition of the Republic was then multiplied exponentially by the nearly unbearable pain that he suffered upon the death of his dear daughter Tullia in February of 45. Once again, as he had done a decade earlier, Cicero took refuge in philosophy and literature; his literary output that resulted during these years was nothing short of remarkable. In 44, he wrote a pair of treatises, *Laelius de amicitia* and *Cato Maior de senectute*, both dedicated to his best friend and confidant, T. Pomponius Atticus, and both set as dialogues (cf. the design of *De oratore*).

The dramatic date of *De amicitia* is 129 BCE. The chief interlocutor is the orator, statesman, and man of letters, Gaius Laelius Sapiens ("the Wise"), named thus for his great learning and knowledge. Laelius is joined in the dialogue by his two sons-in-law, Quintus Mucius Scaevola and Gaius Fannius. Only a few days previous to the discussion, Laelius' most intimate friend, Publius Scipio Africanus Minor (the conqueror of Carthage in 146, prominent statesman, and influential litterateur) had died suddenly and mysteriously. Fannius and Scaevola begin the dialogue by asking Laelius how he is bearing up at the loss of his best friend, a question that provides Laelius with the opportunity to expound at length on the nature and quality of friendship. In this passage, one of the most notable of the dialogue, Laelius praises friendship as one of the gods' greatest gifts to human beings.

1 [19] **mihi perspicere videor** essentially the equivalent of *perspicio*; note that Latin, unlike English, tends to use "seem" personally rather than impersonally: "I seem to myself to see."

natos esse pf. infinitive, from *nascor*; "we've been born"

2 **societas quaedam** Cicero, like Aristotle before him, believed strongly that an innate bond or tie exists among human beings as part and parcel of our nature; this is the subject of the result clause, introduced by *ut*.

maior refers to *societas quaedam*; "greater," i.e., "stronger."

3 **ut** "as"

accederet sc. *ad nos*

3–4 **potiores quam** "preferable to"

4 **alieni** "strangers"

5 **ea** sc. *amicitia*

6 **firmitatis** partitive gen., following *satis* (line 5)

hoc abl. of respect, "herein, in this regard"

praestat "excels," with the dat.

propinquitati "relationship"; the word can refer to relationships between citizens, between neighbors, as well as between members of a family (i.e., relatives).

7 **quod** The clause explicates *hoc* (line 6).

8–9 **sublata . . . benevolentia** abl. absolute, representing most likely a conditional clause

9 **propinquitatis** sc. *nomen*; note the lack of conjs. joining this and the previous clause.

10 [20] **quanta** introduces an indirect question, dependent on *intellegi* (line 11).

11 **quod** The clause explicates *hoc* (line 10); cf. above, line 7.

13 **res** i.e., friendship; "this thing called friendship"

adducta in angustum "reduced, narrowed"

13–14 **ut . . . iungeretur** dependent on *contracta res est et adducta* (line 13); if, as here, the leading verb is pres. pf. in sense, the impf. tense in the result clause will show an on-going action in the pres. time, not in the past; translate "is joined."

15–16 **omnium divinarum humanarumque rerum** Construe as objective gen. with *consensio* (line 17).

16 **cum** "in union with, allied with"

17 **qua** abl. of comparison with *nihil melius* (line 18); "than which"

haud scio an In Cicero the phrase is generally affirmative in nature; "I am inclined to think that, it is probably the case that . . ."

18 **excepta sapientia** abl. absolute; can be idiomatically translated "with the exception of wisdom"

19–20 **alii . . . alii . . . alii . . . alii . . .** "some . . . others . . . others . . . others"

21 **hoc** refers back to *voluptates.*

extremum here = *finis*, i.e., "end, goal in life"; cf. the phrases *finis bonorum* or *summum bonum* (line 24); the reference is to Epicurus and his followers, who maintained that the *summum bonum*, or chief end in life, was the absence of pain and care, i.e., pleasure, *voluptas.*

22 **superiora** i.e., those things mentioned previously, above

caduca et incerta "fleeting and uncertain"

posita i.e., "dependent"

22–23 **non tam . . . quam** "not so much . . . as"

23 **qui** i.e., the Stoic and Peripatetic philosophers

24–25 **praeclare illi** The whole idea in the preceeding clause must be supplied here: "those people [do that] splendidly."

26 **esse** "exist"

27 [21] **iam** continues the line of reasoning; "to proceed."

virtutem i.e., "the word virtue"

27–28 **ex consuetudine vitae sermonisque nostri** i.e., in the way that it is understood in everyday life and speech

28–29 **quidam docti** in particular, the Stoic philosophers, whose definition and concept of virtue was so restrictive and lofty that it practically excluded its attainment by typical human beings

29 **virosque** -*que* here = *sed*

30 **qui habentur** "who are (normally) considered so"

numeremus another hortatory/jussive subjunctive (along with *interpretemur*, line 28, *metiamur*, line 29, and *omittamus*, line 32)

30–31 **Paulos . . . Philos** Latin uses the pl. in such cases to denote the idea of "men like Paulus, etc."

31 **his** "with such men"

34 [22] **tantas** Construe with *quantas* (line 35) in a correlative construction.

opportunitates in the sense of "advantages"

35 **qui** = *quo*, an old form for the abl. of the interrog. and rel. pron.; used here as an adv.: "how"

36 **Ennius** perhaps the greatest of the early Latin poets (239–169 BCE), whose most famous work, *Annales*, an epic written in dactylic hexameters and recounting the history of Rome, is often quoted by Cicero; the poem survives only in fragments.

38 **quicum** = *quocum*; see *qui* above, line 35

39 **qui** "what kind of"

esset impf. subjunctive in the apodosis (conclusion) of a contrary-to-fact, pres. condition (posed as a question)

tantus here, equivalent to *magnus*

fructus "enjoyment"

40 **haberes qui** Note the absence of the antecedent.

illis refers back to *prosperis rebus* (line 39).

ac "as"; *ac* or *atque* is often used with adjs. and advs. that express *likeness.*

41 **adversas** sc. *res*

sine eo prepositional phrase that introduces a rel. clause functioning as the protasis of a contrary-to-fact condition

43 **quae expetuntur** i.e., things that are objects of desire

43–44 **opportunae sunt singulae rebus fere singulis** distributive: "are, for the most part, suited individually for individual things"

44–46 **utare . . . colare . . . laudere . . . fungare** Note the *-re* ending for *–ris.*

46 **careas . . . fungare** Both verbs take the abl.

46–49 Note the several short phrases, coming one upon the other, without the use of connecting particles (ASYNDETON).

47 **verteris** fut. pf., illustrating more precisely than would English the temporal relationship of the subordinate verb to the main verb

49 **non aqua, non igni** In antiquity, water and fire were considered the first necessities of life, so much so that the typical Roman decree of exile was expressed by means of a prohibition from offering the person in question fire and water; both words are in the abl. case, as objects of *utimur* (line 50).

50 **locis pluribus** abl. of place where

51 **de vulgari aut de mediocri** sc. *amicitia*

52 **de vera et perfecta** i.e., the true and faultless kinds of friendship, only few of which have become renowned (cf. *qui pauci nominantur*, line 53); these are the ideal friendships that can exist only between the wise and the good.

53 **qualis** sc. *talis* as antecedent

55 **partiens communicansque** almost synonymous, "by dividing and sharing"; the pples. modify *amicitia* (line 54); note the CHIASTIC arrangement (ABBA) of the acc. adjs. (*adversas . . . leviores*) surrounding the nom. pples.

56 [23] **cumque** "while, seeing that . . ."

commoditates close in sense to *opportunitates* (above, line 34)

57 **illa** abl. of respect; sc. *commoditate* (cf. *hoc*, above, line 6)

58 **quod . . . posterum** elaborates on *illa* [*commoditate*] (line 57): "in that/because it offers/sheds the light of good hope for the future."

60 **tamquam** softens the idea contained in *exemplar aliquod . . . sui* (lines 60–61).

61 **sui** gen., dependent on *exemplar aliquod*

61–63 **quocirca . . . vivunt** a series of four clauses containing intentional oxymorons (apparent contradictions in terms), each introduced by *et* (POLYSYNDETON)

62 **dictu** supine in *-u* with a compar. adj.

64 **amicorum** subjective gen. dependent on *honos, memoria, desiderium* (line 63); translate, "on the part of their friends"

ex quo = *ex qua re*; "on account of which"

64–65 **illorum . . . horum** i.e., the departed/dead . . . the survivors; note the CHIASMUS of *beata mors . . . vita laudabilis.*

65–68 **quod si . . . permanebit** a good example of a fut. more vivid condition

69 **quanta . . . sit** indirect question introduced by *percipi potest* (line 70)

70–71 **quae . . . quae . . . quae** The first two are interrog. adjs., the third a rel. pron. equivalent to *ut ea.*

73 **boni** partitive gen.

De officiis 1.134–137

De officiis (*On* [*Moral*] *Duties*), Cicero's last work on moral philosophy, was composed (rather hastily) during the final months of 44 BCE. At that time, Cicero once again found himself deeply embroiled in affairs of state: in September 44, he had launched a series of speeches, known as the *Philippics*, against Mark Antony; it was these orations that would ultimately prove responsible for Cicero's proscription and murder a year later, on December 7, 43 BCE.

The treatise is addressed ostensibly to Cicero's son, Marcus, who was then twenty-one years old and studying philosophy abroad in Athens. In the preface, Cicero explains his motivation for writing and his choice of subject matter (1.4):

> But since I had decided to write something to you now (and much more in the future), I wanted especially to begin with something that was particularly suitable to your age and to my authority. For while many important and useful matters in philosophy have been fully and accurately discussed by philosophers, it is

> their teachings handed down on the subject of moral duties that seem to have the widest application. Indeed, no part of life, neither in public affairs nor in private, neither in the forum nor at home, neither when you are acting on your own nor when you are dealing with another, can be free from moral duty. All that is honorable in life depends upon its cultivation; and all that is morally base upon its neglect.

Modeled on a second-century BCE work by the Greek Stoic philosopher Panaetius of Rhodes, *On Duty (Peri tou kathekontos)*, *De officiis* consists of three books. The first deals with *honestum* (the honorable or what is morally right), the second with *utile* (the useful or expedient), and the third with the question of how to deal with situations in which the honorable comes into conflict with the useful. Given the date and circumstances surrounding its composition, it is not surprising to find the content and mood of the work colored heavily by the current political situation following upon the assassination of Julius Caesar. In any case, *De officiis* became one of Cicero's most influential works in subsequent ages; during the Enlightenment, English speakers often referred to it affectionately as "Tully's Offices."

The present selection is excerpted from Book 1, wherein Cicero describes the four cardinal virtues (prudence, temperance, justice, and fortitude). He argues that "propriety" or "seemliness" (*decorum*), an element of temperance, is inseparable from the whole of honorableness or moral goodness, and that the power of speech, both oratory and conversation, is a significant element in the attainment of propriety. The rules for "seemly conversation" that he presents here apply equally well to civil discourse in our own times.

1–2 [134] **sit . . . insit** Cicero employs the hortatory (jussive) subjunctive extensively in this paragraph as he begins his instruction concerning appropriate conversation; this mode of exhortation is continued subsequently through multiple uses of the passive periphrastic construction (showing obligation or necessity) followed by jussive noun clauses (i.e., substantive clauses of result).

1 **sermo** "conversation"

Socratici Cicero mentions Plato's Socrates earlier (1.108) and elsewhere (e.g., *De oratore* 2.270) as an example of a genial, witty, and refined conversationalist; students of Socrates, e.g., Plato and Xenophon, would be counted among this group.

2–5 **nec vero . . . putet** The subject of this sentence, i.e., the person engaged in conversation, must be inferred from the word *sermo* in the previous sentence.

3 **tamquam in possessionem suam venerit** i.e., as if he has taken possession of his own property

4 **cum reliquis in rebus tum** "as in other things, so especially"

5 **vicissitudinem** "interchange, alternation"; i.e., each one taking his own turn

non iniquam an example of the rhetorical device, LITOTES, affirming something by denying its opposite

in primis "especially, above all"

6 **si seriis** i.e., *de rebus seriis*; here Cicero's concern is that conversation be appropriate (*quid decet*) to the subject.

7–11 **in primisque . . . dicitur** The conversationalist must especially take care that his comments and behavior do not reveal some flaw in character (*in moribus*, line 8).

9 **studiose** here, "deliberately, on purpose"

detrahendi causa "in order to disparage them, detract from their characters"

10 **per ridiculum aut severe** i.e., whether in jest or in seriousness

11 **dicitur** modified by the advs. *maledice contumelioseque* (line 10), an example of the impers. use of the pass. voice; we would in such cases generally employ the act. voice: "[when] someone speaks . . ."

12 [135] **de re publica** i.e., about political topics, politics

13 **danda . . . opera est** *operam dare* = "to work hard at, pay attention to, take care to"; pass. periphrastic (second periphrastic conjugation) here introducing a jussive noun (substantive clause of result) clause, *ut . . . revocetur* (lines 13–14)

14 **ad haec** "to the subject at hand"

oratio = *sermo*

14–15 **†utcumque aderunt†** Editors have not been able to agree on a suitable emendation of this difficult text, though Shackleton Bailey, *BMCR* 6 (1995) 260, has suggested that the text as transmitted might stand: "Conversation has certain staple topics. It may diverge to others, but must come back to these, 'but in whatever way they crop up.' They will not always present themselves (*aderunt*) in the same form."

16 **animadvertendum est** pass. periphrastic used impersonally (literally, "it must be observed/noticed [by us]"), introducing here an indirect question, *quatenus . . . habeat* (line 17); translate, "we must observe . . ."

17 **quatenus** "how far, the extent to which"

17–18 **ut . . . ita** "just as . . . so"

19–21 [136] **quomodo . . . sic** "just as . . . so"; cf. *ut . . . ita*, lines 17–18

20 **praecipitur** impers. use of the pass., introducing a jussive noun clause (*ut . . . fugiamus*); translate, "we are instructed/advised . . . to avoid . . ."

id est introducing a clause that explicates more clearly the word *perturbationes*; cf. our use of the abbreviation "i.e."; *motus animi* is the normal term for "emotions, passions."

21 **motibus** abl. of separation with *vacare* (line 22)

optemperantes pple., modifying *motus animi nimios* (lines 20–21) and governing the dat., *rationi*

22–23 **aut . . . aut . . . aut . . . aut . . . aut** The repeated use of conjs. to join a series of words is the rhetorical device known as POLYSYNDETON (opposite of ASYNDETON).

22 **exsistat** "show itself"

24 **curandum est** impers. use of the pass. periphrastic (cf. *animadvertendum est*, line 16), introducing a jussive noun clause, *ut . . . videamur* (lines 24–25); translate, "we must take care to . . ."

sermonem conferemus i.e., converse, share conversation; note the use of the fut. rather than the subjunctive, which might have been employed in a subordinate clause within another subjunctive clause.

25 **videamur** "we may be seen"

26–27 **utendum est** cf. *curandum est* (above, line 24); translate "we must use, employ"; as one would expect of objects of *utor*; *contentione* (line 27) and *gravitate* (line 28) are in the abl. case.

28 **agendum** sc. *est*

29 **ut . . . sic** "just as . . . so"; cf. lines 17–18 (*ut . . . ita*) and 20–21

ad urendum et secandum "to cauterization and amputation"; medical procedures employed only in extreme cases, and to prevent a wound or disease from overtaking the entire body

33 [137] **magnam . . . partem** adverbial, "for the most part, in most cases"

clementi castigatione i.e., gentle reproof/criticism

34 **gravitate . . . adiuncta** abl. absolute; *gravitas*: "seriousness, earnestness"

et . . . et "both . . . and"

35 **contumelia** "abusive language"

35–36 **illud ipsum quod acerbitatis habet obiurgatio** = *illud ipsum acerbitatis quod habet obiurgatio*; *acerbitatis* is partitive gen.

36 **obiurgatio** "chiding, reproof"

ipsius Construe with *causa* as a preceding gen.; it is the antecedent of the rel. clause, *qui obiurgetur*, line 37.

id This pron. is technically redundant; it refers to *illud ipsum . . . acerbitatis* (line 35), subject of *esse susceptum* (line 37), the verb in indirect discourse.

39–40 **retinere . . . pellere** Both infinitives are dependent on *rectum est*, line 37.

40 **quae** rel. pron. preceding its antecedent *ea* in line 41

cum aliqua pertubatione "with some degree of agitation/excitement"

41 **constanter** adv., "with constancy," i.e., steadily, calmly, with consistency of character

iis qui adsunt "by those who are present," i.e., those who witness, bystanders; *iis* is dat. case, regularly used with the pass. infinitive *probari* (line 42) to mean "to appear worthy of approval to."

42 **deforme . . . est** "it is tasteless/disgusting"

43 **cum inrisione audientium** "amid the ridicule of one's listeners"

43–44 **militem gloriosum** "the braggart soldier," a stock character in new Attic comedy and Roman comedy; Cicero probably has in mind Pyrgopolynices, the title character in Plautus' *Miles Gloriosus*, or Thraso in Terence's *Eunuchus*.

Appendix A

- *Map of the Roman World in the Time of Cicero*
- *Map of Italy*

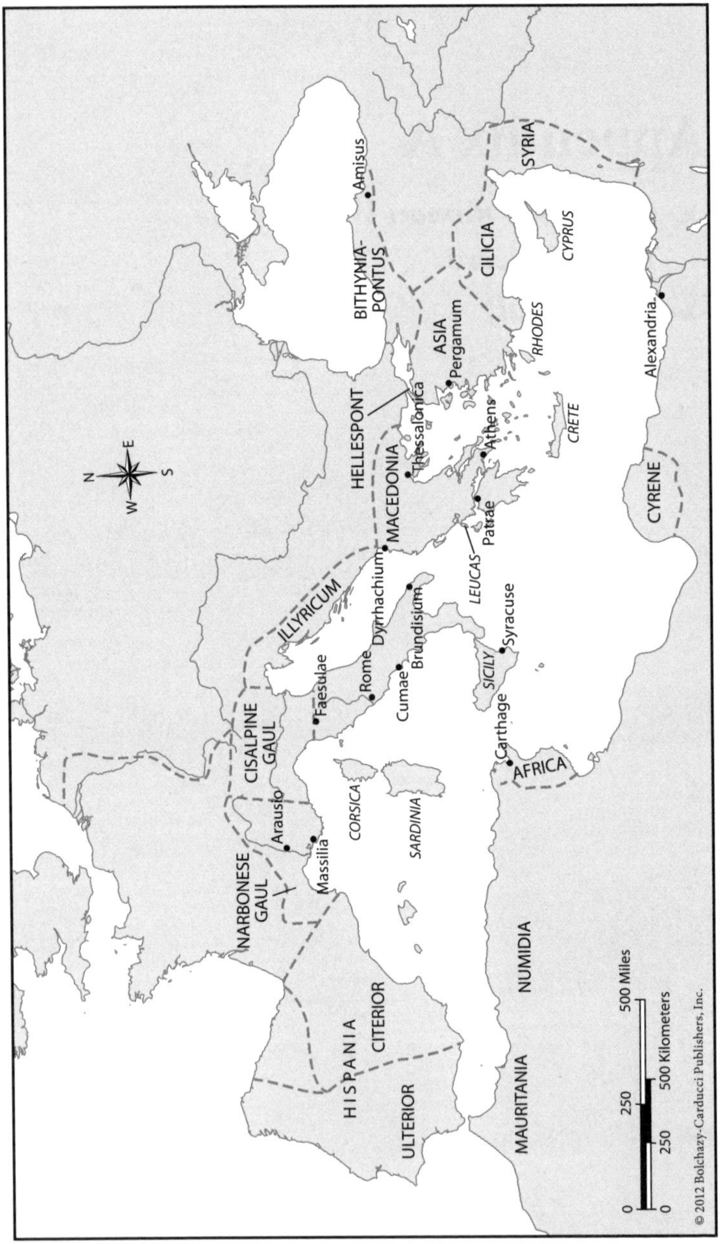
N
E
S
W
Amisus
SYRIA
CYPRUS
CILICIA
BITHYNIA-PONTUS
ASIA
Pergamum
RHODES
Alexandria
HELLESPONT
Thessalonica
Athens
CRETE
MACEDONIA
Patrae
CYRENE
LEUCAS
Dyrrhachium
ILLYRICUM
Brundisium
Syracuse
Rome
Cumae
SICILY
Faesulae
CISALPINE GAUL
Carthage
AFRICA
Arausio
Massilia
CORSICA
SARDINIA
NARBONESE GAUL
NUMIDIA
HISPANIA
CITERIOR
ULTERIOR
MAURITANIA
0
250
500 Miles
0
250
500 Kilometers
© 2012 Bolchazy-Carducci Publishers, Inc.

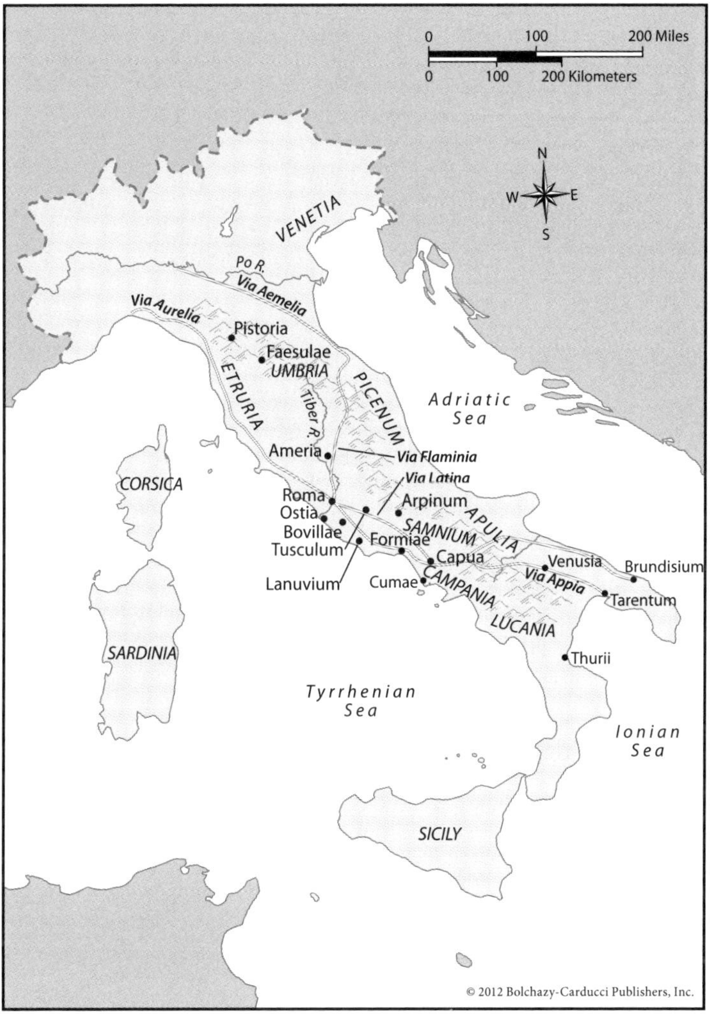

0
100
200 Miles
0
100
200 Kilometers
N
W
E
S
VENETIA
Po R.
Via Aemelia
Via Aurelia
Pistoria
Faesulae
UMBRIA
ETRURIA
Tiber R.
PICENUM
Adriatic Sea
CORSICA
Ameria
Via Flaminia
Via Latina
Roma
Ostia
Bovillae
Tusculum
Lanuvium
Arpinum
APULIA
SAMNIUM
Formiae
Capua
Cumae
CAMPANIA
Venusia
Via Appia
Brundisium
Tarentum
LUCANIA
Thurii
SARDINIA
Tyrrhenian Sea
Ionian Sea
SICILY

Appendix B

~ *Significant Events During Cicero's Lifetime*

(All dates are BCE)

106	Birth of Marcus Tullius Cicero (3 January) and of Cn. Pompeius Magnus (Pompey the Great) (September)
104	Marius, consul for the second time, reorganizes Roman army
100	Marius, consul for the sixth time; birth of C. Julius Caesar (July)
95	Lucius Licinius Crassus and Quintus Mucius Scaevola Pontifex consuls
91–87	Social War (War with Italian Allies); Cicero assumes *toga virilis*; serves under Pompeius Strabo (89) and Sulla (88); writes *De inventione*
88	Cicero meets Philo of Larissa, head of Academy, who had fled to Rome; Sulla occupies Rome; Marius flees and joins L. Cornelius Cinna
88–85	First Mithridatic War
87	Marius and consul Cinna seize Rome while Sulla fights in Greece; proscriptions
86	Marius, consul for the seventh time, dies in office
85	Sulla concludes peace with Mithridates
84	Cinna, consul for the fourth time, killed in mutiny

83–81	Second Mithridatic War
82	Civil War; Sulla siezes Rome and is named dictator (82–81); proscriptions
81	Sulla as dictator reforms constitution, including establishment of 7 standing criminal courts with senatorial juries; Cicero's *Pro Quinctio*
80	Cicero's *Pro Roscio Amerino*
79	Sulla resigns dictatorship; birth of Cicero's daughter, Tullia (?)
79–77	Cicero travels to Athens, Rhodes, and Asia Minor; studies with Molon of Rhodes
78	Sulla dies
75	Cicero serves as quaestor in Western Sicily; becomes a member of the Senate
74–63	Third Mithridatic War; Lucullus given command against Mithridates
73–71	Verres governor of Sicily; Spartacus leads slave rebellion and is defeated by Pompey and Crassus; Cicero's *Pro Roscio comoedo* (*c.* 72); *Pro Tullio* (71)
70	First consulship of Pompey and Crassus; Trial of Verres; Cicero's *Divinatio in Caecilium, In Verrem*; *Lex Aurelia* changes constitution of juries to two-thirds equestrian
69	Cicero serves as aedile; Cicero's *Pro Fonteio; Pro Caecina*
67	Lucullus relieved of Mithridatic command; *Lex Gabinia* gives Pompey command against pirates
66	Cicero serves as praetor, presides over extortion court; Cicero's *Pro lege Manilia*; *Lex Manilia* gives Pompey Mithridatic command; Cicero's *Pro Cluentio*
65	Birth of Cicero's son, Marcus

63	Cicero serves as consul; Cicero's *De lege agraria, Pro Rabirio perduellionis reo*; conspiracy of Catiline; Cicero's *In Catilinam, Pro Murena*; execution of the conspirators (5 December); Metellus Nepos attacks Cicero (10 December); death of Mithridates; Pompey organizes campaign in the East
62	Defeat and death of Catiline; Cicero's *Pro Sulla, Pro Archia*; Bona Dea scandal (Clodius) in Caesar's house; Pompey returns to Italy and disbands army
61	Senate opposes Pompey and Crassus; Clodius acquitted of sacrilege through bribery
60	Formation of "First Triumvirate"
59	Caesar serves as consul; Pompey marries Caesar's daughter Julia; *Lex Vatinia* gives Caesar command of Cisalpine Gaul and Illyricum, the Senate adds Transalpine Gaul; Clodius adopted into a plebeian family; Cicero's *Pro Flacco*
58	L. Calpurnius Piso and Aulus Gabinius serve as consuls; Clodius as tribune; Cato sent to annex Cyprus; Cicero exiled; Caesar in Gaul defeats Helvetii and Ariovistus
57	Cicero returns to Rome (4 September); Cicero's *Post reditum in senatu, Post reditum ad quirites, De domo sua*; Pompey commissioner for grain supply
56	Cicero attempts to break up the "triumvirate"; Cicero's *Pro Sestio, In Vatinium, Pro Caelio*; Conference at Luca (May) reaffirms "triumvirate"; Cicero's "palinode"; Cicero's *De haruspicum responso, De provinciis consularibus, Pro Balbo*
55	Pompey and Crassus consuls for the second time; Caesar's command in Gaul extended for another five years; Cicero's *In Pisonem, De oratore*

54	Cicero defends Vatinius; Cicero's *Pro Scauro, Pro Plancio;* Cicero defends Gabinius; death of Pompey's wife Julia, daughter of Caesar; Cicero's *De republica* (54–51), *De legibus* (begun about this time), *Partitiones oratoriae* (54–52 or 45–44), *Pro Rabirio Postumo* (or 53)
53	Crassus defeated and killed by the Parthians at Carrhae; Cicero co-opted into the College of Augurs; rioting between gangs of Clodius and Milo
52	Murder of Clodius (18 January) by Milo, followed by riots and burning of senate house; Pompey appointed sole consul; trial of Milo and Cicero's *Pro Milone*
51–50	Cicero serves as governor of Cilicia
49	Caesar crosses Rubicon (10 January), Civil War; Pompey leaves Italy (17 March); Caesar visits Cicero (28 March); Cicero follows Pompey to Greece (7 June); Caesar dictator, defeats Pompey's army in Spain
48	Pompey defeated at Pharsalus (9 August) and subsequently murdered in Egypt; Caesar in Egypt; Cicero returns to Brundisium
47	Caesar in Egypt, Syria, and Asia; returns to Italy (September) and pardons Cicero
46	Pompeian forces defeated at Thapsus; Cato commits suicide; Cicero divorces Terentia; Cicero's *Brutus, Paradoxa Stoicorum, Cato, Orator, Pro Marcello, Pro Ligario*
45	Pompey's sons defeated at Munda (March); Caesar's *Anticato*; death of Cicero's daughter, Tullia; Cicero's *De finibus bonorum et malorum, Academica, Tusculanae disputationes, De natura deorum, Pro rege Deiotaro*

44 Caesar *dictator perpetuus* (February); assassinated (15 March); Octavian named Caesar's heir; falling out between Cicero and Antony; Cicero assumes unofficial leadership of Senate and makes pact with Octavian; Cicero's *De senectute, De amicitia, De divinatione, De fato, Topica, Philippics* 1–4, *De officiis*

43 Civil War; Cicero's *Philippics* 5–14; Antony defeated at Mutina (April) by Octavian and consuls Hirtius and Pansa (consuls are killed); Antonians declared public enemies; Octavian occupies Rome, elected consul, outlaws Caesar's assassins; forms "Second Triumvirate" with Antony and Lepidus (November); proscriptions; murder of Cicero (7 December)

Complete Vocabulary

ā *or* **ab,** *prep.+ abl.,* from, away from; by (*agent*)
abdō, -ere, -didī, -ditum, to put away, withdraw, remove, hide
abeō, -īre, -iī, -itum, to go away, retire, pass away
aberrō (1), to wander, deviate
absens, -entis, *adj.,* absent
absolvō, -ere, -solvī, -solutum, to loosen, free, acquit
abstrahō, -ere, -traxī, -tractum, to drag away
absum, abesse, āfuī, to be away, absent, distant
abundō (1), to overflow
ac. *See* **atque**
accēdō, -ere, -cessī, -cessum, to approach
accīdō, -ere, -cīdī, -cisum, to hack at, weaken, ruin
accipiō, -ere, -cēpī, -ceptum, to take, receive, accept, hear
accūrātē, *adv.,* accurately, exactly, carefully
accūsō (1), to accuse, blame, find fault with
ācer, ācris, ācre, *adj.,* fierce, keen, sharp
acerbitas, -ātis, *f.,* harshness, bitterness
acerbus, -a, -um, *adj.,* bitter, harsh, rough, severe
actio, -ōnis, *f.,* action, doing; *in rhetorical terms,* delivery of a speech
acuō, -ere, -uī, -ūtum, to sharpen, practice
ad, *prep.+ acc.,* to, towards
addūcō, -ere, -duxī, -ductum, to draw to
adferō, adferre, attulī, adlatum, to carry, bring to
adficiō, -ere, -fēcī, -fectum, to affect in any way, influence
adfirmō (1), to affirm, strengthen, assert as true
adhibeō, -ēre, -uī, -itum, to apply, bring to
adhūc, *adv.,* up to the present time, thus far
adiūmentum, -ī, *n.,* help, assistance
adiungō, -ere, -iunxī, -iunctum, to join to
adiuvō, -āre, -iūvī, -iūtum, to help assist, support

administrō (1), to help, assist, mangage, direct
adorior, -īrī, -ortus sum, to attack
adsum, -esse, -fuī, —, to be present, be here
adulescentia, -ae, *f.*, youth
adulter, -erī, *m.*, an adulterer
adversārius, -a, -um, *adj.*, turned toward, opposed
adversārius, -ī, *m.*, rival, adversary
adversus, -a, -um, *adj.*, opposite, facing; adverse
advertō, -ere, -vertī, -versum, to turn toward, direct, direct one's attention
aedificō (1), to build, create, establish
aequālis, -e, *adj.*, even
aequē, *adv.*, in like manner, equally
aequitās, -ātis, *f.*, fairness, justice
aequus, -a, -um, *adj.*, equal, even
aerārium, -ī, *n.*, the public treasury
aerumna, -ae, *f.*, toil, labor, hardship
aetās, -ātis, *f.*, age, generation
Āfricānus, -a, -um, *adj.*, belonging to Africa; *as a name*, referring to Publius Scipio Africanus Minor, the conqueror of Carthage in 146 BCE, prominent statesman, and influential man of letters
ager, agrī, *m.*, field, countryside
agō, -ere, ēgī, actum, to act, do; to drive
agrestis, -e, *adj.*, belonging to the country, rustic
āiō, *defective verb,* to say
āleātor, -ōris, *m.*, a dice player, gambler
aliēnus, -a, -um, *adj.*, belonging to another, foreign
aliquī, aliquae, aliquod, *adj.*, some, any
aliquis, aliquid, *pron.*, someone, something, anyone, anything
alius, -a, -ud, *adj.*, another, other
alō, -ere, aluī, altum, to nourish, support
alter, -era, -erum, *pron.*, one (of two), the other
altum, -ī, *n.*, height; depth; the deep sea
alveolus, -ī, *m.*, a gaming board
amans, -antis, *adj.*, loving, affectionate, fond of
āmentia, -ae, *f.*, insanity, madness, folly
amiciō, -īre, -icuī, -ictum, to clothe, wrap round
amīcitia, -ae, *f.*, friendship
amīcus, -a, -um, *adj.*, friendly, well-wishing, inclined, favorable to
amīcus, -ī, *m.*, a friend
āmittō, -ere, -mīsī, -missum, to send away, let go
amō (1), to love

amor, -ōris, *m.*, love, passion, desire
amplus, -a, -um, *adj.*, large, ample; important, eminent
an, *conj.*, or, or whether
ancilla, -ae, *f.*, a female slave
angō, -ere, —, —, to hurt, distress
angustum, -ī, *n.*, a narrow space; difficulty
anima, -ae, *f.*, wind, breath, life, the rational soul
animadvertō, -ere, -vertī, -versum, to take notice of
animus, -ī, *m.*, mind, spirit
annus, -ī, *m.*, year
ante, *adv.*, before
antelūcānus, -a, -um, *adj.*, happening before daybreak; thus, can imply "lasting all night long"
antīquitās, -ātis, *f.*, antiquity, ancient times
apertē, *adv.*, openly
apparō (1), to prepare, get ready
appellō (1), to address, speak to
Appennīnus, -ī, *m.*, the Appennines, the mountain range running down through Italy
apud, *prep. + acc.*, at, near, in the presence of, at one's house
aqua, -ae, *f.*, water
arbitrātus, -ūs, *m.*, will, choice, wish, approval
arbitror, -ārī, arbitrātus sum, to perceive, judge, think
arma, -ōrum, *n. pl.*, weapons
armō (1), to arm, equip
ars, artis, *f.*, art, skill, craft
aspectus, -ūs, *m.*, sight, view, range of vision, aspect
assuēfaciō, -ere, -fēcī, -factum, to accustom to
at, *conj.*, but, moreover
atque, *conj.*, and
attingō, -ere, -tigī, -tactum, to touch, reach, border upon
auctōritās, -ātis, *f.*, power, authority
audācia, -ae, *f.*, boldness, impudence, temerity
audax, -ācis, *adj.*, audacious, bold, courageous, rash
audeō, -ēre, ausus sum, to dare
audiō, -īre, -īvī, -ītum, to hear
augeō, -ēre, auxī, auctum, to increase
augur, -uris, *m.*, augur, a member of the Priestly College of Augurs, official Roman diviners who advised the Senate and magistrates concerning signs indicating the will of the gods
auris, -is, *f.*, the ear
aut, *conj.*, or; **aut . . . aut,** either. . .or
autem, *conj.*, but, on the other hand, however, moreover
āvocō (1), to call away

balineum, -ī, *n.*, a bath, bathing place
barbarus, -a, -um, *adj.*, foreign, barbarian

barbātus, -a, -um, *adj.*, bearded
beātus, -a, -um, *adj.*, blessed, happy
bellum, -ī, *n.*, war
bellus, -a, -um, *adj.*, pretty, handsome, charming
bēlua, -ae, *f.*, a beast
bene, *adv.*, well, in a good way
benevolentia, -ae, *f.*, good-will, kindness
bonus, -a, -um, *adj.*, good
brevis, -e, *adj.*, short, brief, concise
brevitās, -ātis, *f.*, shortness

cadō, -ere, cecidī, cāsum, to fall
cadūcus, -a, -um, *adj.*, fallen, falling
caedēs, -is, *f.*, slaughter, bloodshed
caedō, -ere, cecīdī, caesum, to cut down, slaughter
Caesar, -āris, *m.*, a Roman family name of the *gens Julia*; the most famous member was C. Julius Caesar, contemporary of Cicero, general and later dictator, assassinated on the Ides of March, 44 BCE
calamitās, -ātis, *f.*, misfortune, damage
calceus, -ī, *m.*, a shoe
cānescō, -ere, —, —, to become white; to become old
cantō (1), to sing, play
capillus, -ī, *m.*, the hair of the head or beard
capiō, -ere, cēpī, captum, to take, capture; to conceive; to contain
carcer, -eris, *m.*, a prison, jail, cell
careō, -ēre, -uī, -itūrus, + *abl.*, to lack, be without
cāritas, -ātis, *f.*, dearness, affection
cārus, -a, -um, *adj.*, high-priced, dear
castīgātio, -ōnis, *f.*, punishment, reproof
castīgō (1), to reprove, check
castra, -ōrum, *n. pl.*, camp
Catilīna, -ae, *m.*, L. Sergius Catiline, a Roman of noble birth who masterminded a conspiracy against the Roman state during Cicero's consulship in 63 BCE
Cato, -ōnis, *m.*, Roman cognomen of the *gens Porcia*; its two most famous members were M. Porcius Cato Censorius [the Elder] (234–149 BCE) and M. Porcius Cato Uticensis [the Younger], contemporary of Cicero, who committed suicide in 46 BCE
causa, -ae, *f.*, cause, reason
celebritas, -ātis, *f.*, frequenting in large numbers, crowdedness; renown
celebrō (1), to visit frequently, *or* in large numbers
celeritās, -ātis, *f.*, quickness, swiftness

cēna, -ae, *f.*, a meal, dinner
certāmen, -inis, *n.*, a contest, a struggle
certē, *adv.*, certainly, assuredly; at least, at any rate
certō (1), to struggle, contend
certus, -a, -um, *adj.*, certain, fixed
cēterus, -a, -um, *adj.*, the rest, remaining; usually found in the pl., **cēterī, -ae, -a**
Cicero, -ōnis, *m.*, Roman cognomen of the *gens Tullia*, whose most notable members were M. Tullius Cicero, great orator and statesman who was murdered in 43 BCE, his younger brother Quintus, and his son Marcus
Cilicia, -ae, *f.*, a region in Asia Minor
cīvīlis, -e, *adj.*, civil, of a citizen
cīvis, -is, *m.* or *f.*, citizen
cīvitās, -ātis, *f.*, a union of citizens, a state, commonwealth
clārus, -a, -um, *adj.*, clear, bright; famous
classis, -is, *f.*, a fleet of ships
clēmens, -entis, *adj.*, mild, kind
Clōdius, -ī, *m.*, Publius Clodius Pulcher, tribune of the people, Cicero's adversary, who instigated his exile and was later killed in a scuffle with Milo in 52 BCE
coepiō, -ere, coepī, coeptum, to begin (pres. tenses used very rarely)
cōgitātio, -ōnis, *f.*, thinking
cōgitō (1), to turn over in the mind, to think, reflect, consider
cognitio, -ōnis, *f.*, getting to know, study; knowledge or acquaintance with a person or thing
cognoscō, -ere, -gnōvī, -gnitum, to get to know, learn
cōgō, -ere, coēgī, coactum, to gather together, force, compel, compress, restrain
cohors, -tis, *f.*, a troop, cohort
colligō, -ere, -lēgī, -lēctum, to collect, gather up, concentrate
Collīnus, -a, -um, of or on the Quirinal hill in Rome; *Tribus Collina* was the name of one of the city tribes of Rome
colō, -ere, coluī, cultum, to cultivate, tend; to pay constant attention to, cultivate the friendship of, devote oneself to
colōnia, -ae, *f.*, a colony; farm, estate
comes, -itis, *m.*, companion
comitātus, -ūs, *m.*, a retinue, following
comitia, -ōrum, *n. pl.*, the assembly of the Roman people for the election of magistrates, the elections

committō, -ere, -mīsī, -missum, to unite, connect, commit (a crime)

commode, *adv.*,rightly, properly, comfortably, pleasantly

commoditās, -ātis, *f.*, convenience, advantage; proportion, symmetry

commodus, -a, -um, *adj.*, proper, satisfactory

commoror, -ārī, -ātus sum, to linger, remain

commūnicō (1), to share, divide out

commūnis, -e, *adj.*, shared, common, general

comparō (1), to prepare, get ready, provide

competītor, -ōris, *m.*, a rival, competitor

complector, -ī, complexus sum, to embrace, grasp, comprehend

complexus, -ūs, *m.*, an embrace

complures, complura, *adj.*, very many

comprehendō, -ere, -prehendī, -prehensum, to grasp; to comprehend, perceive

concēdō, -ere, -cessī, -cessum, to go away, retire, withdraw

concīdō, -ere, -cīdī, -cīsum, to cut up, cut in pieces, cut down, strike down

conciliō (1), to bring together, unite, connect

concordia, -ae, *f.*, harmony, concord

conferō, -ferre, -tulī, -lātum, to bring together, join, meet

conficiō, -ere, -fēcī, -fectum, to bring about, accomplish; to wear out, use up, exhaust

confīdō, -ere, -fīsus sum, to have complete trust, be assured

confirmō (1), to make firm, confirm, strengthen

conflīgō, -ere, -flixī, -flictum, to throw together, bring together; to collide, clash

conformātio, -ōnis, *f.*, forming, form, shape

conformō (1), to form, put together

confugiō, -ere, -fūgī, —, to fly to, take refuge with

coniunctio, -ōnis, *f.*, uniting

coniunctus, -a, -um, *adj.*, connected, joined, allied

coniungō, -ere, -iunxī, -iunctum, to join together

conlēga, -ae, *m.*, a colleague, partner in office

conlēgium, -ī, *n.*, colleagueship; college

conligō, -ere, -lēgī, -lectum, to gather together, bring together, collect

conlocō (1), to place, set

conquiescō, -ere, -quiēvī, -quiētum, to take rest, repose

conscrībō, -ere, -scripsī, -scriptum, to enter on a list, enroll

consensio, -ōnis, *f.*, agreement, harmony, consent
consensus, -ūs, *m.*, agreement, unanimity, concord
consequor, -ī, consecūtus sum, to follow, go after
conservō (1), to keep, preserve
consīderātē, *adv.*, carefully, thoughtfully
consīderō (1), to look at, regard carefully, contemplate
consilium, -ī, *n.*, a deliberation, consultation, counsel
consors, -sortis, *m.*, consort, partner
constanter, *adv.*, steadily, firmly
constantia, -ae, *f.*, steadiness, firmness
constituō, -ere, -stituī, -stitūtum, to set up, place, establish
constō, -āre, -stitī, -stātum, to stand together, consist; depend upon
constructio, -ōnis, *f.*, a putting together, construction
consuētūdo, -inis, *f.*, custom, usage, habit
consul, -ulis, *m.*, consul, the chief magistrate in Rome; two consuls were elected annually to hold office for a year; consuls had both military and civil powers
consulātus, -ūs, *m.*, the consulship
consulō, -ere, -suluī, -sultum, to consult, consider, deliberate, weigh
consūmō, -ere, -sumpsī, -sumptum, to spend, employ; to take altogether, consume
contendō, -ere, -tendī, -tentum, to contend; to strain, exert
contentio, -ōnis, *f.*, exertion, effort, striving
continens, -entis, *adj.*, self-controlled, continent; hanging together
continentia, -ae, *f.*, self-control, moderation
contineō, -ēre, -tinuī, -tentum, to keep, hold, hold fast
contio, -ōnis, *f.*, a public meeting
contrā, *prep.+ acc.*, against, opposite, face to face
contrahō, -ere, -traxī, -tractum, to draw together, unite, contract
contubernālis, -is, *m.* or *f.*, one who shares the same tent, a messmate; comrade, supporter
contumēlia, -ae, *f.*, insult, affront
contumēliōsē, *adv.*, abusively
convalescō, -ere, -valuī, —, to become strong
convīcium, -ī, *n.*, a loud cry, shout, clamor
convīvium, -ī, *n.*, a feast, entertainment, banquet
convocō (1), to call together, assemble
cooptō (1), to choose, elect

cōpia, -ae, *f.*, plenty, abundance; *pl.*, troops, forces
corpus, -oris, *n.*, body
cotīdiānus, -a, -um, *adj.*, of every day, daily
cotīdiē, *adv.*, daily, every day
Crassipes, -edis, *m.*, Furius Crassipes, the second husband of Cicero's daughter, Tullia
crescō, -ere, crēvī, crētum, to grow, increase
crīmen, -inis, *n.*, accusation, charge
cruciātus, -ūs, *m.*, torture, torment
culpa, -ae, *f.*, error, fault
cultus, -ūs, *m.*, cultivation, care
cum, *conj.*, when, since, although
cum, *prep.+ abl.*, with
cumulātus, -a, -um, *adj.*, heaped up, increased, enlarged; perfected
cunctor (1), to delay, hesitate
cunctus, -a, -um, *adj.*, all, entire
cupiditās, -ātis, *f.*, eager desire, passion
cupidus, -a, -um, *adj.*, desirous, eager
cupiō, -ere, -īvī *or* **-iī, -ītum,** desire, wish for, long for
cūr, *interr. adv.*, why?
cūra, -ae, *f.*, care, concern
cūrātio, -ōnis, *f.*, attention, care, medical care, healing
Cūrius, -ī, *m.*, M.' Curius, a Roman businessman living in Patrae, and a friend to Atticus and Cicero
cūrō (1), to care for, attend to
cursus, -ūs, *m.*, course, path, journey
custōs, -ōdis, *m.*, a guard

dē, *prep.+ abl.*, about, down from
dēbeō, -ēre, -uī, -itum, to owe, be obliged to
dēbilis, -e, *adj.*, powerless, feeble, weak
dēbilitas, -tātis, *f.*, feebleness, weakness
dēbilitō (1), to weaken, disable
dēcēdō, -ere, -cessī, -cessum, to move away
December, -bris, bre, *adj.*, belonging to the month December; **mensis December,** December
dēclārō (1), to make clear, reveal, declare, proclaim
dēcurrō, -ere, -currī, -cursum, to run down, hurry down, sail down
dēdō, -ere, -didī, -ditum, to dedicate, devote; to surrender
dēdūcō, -ere, -duxī, -ductum, to lead down
dēfatīgō (1), to fatigue, weary, tire
dēfendō, -ere, -fendī, -fensum, to repel, repulse, defend
dēferō, -ferre, -tulī, -lātum, to bring, carry; to report, tell

dēfessus, -a, -um, *adj.*, weary, tired
dēficiō, -ere, -fēcī, -fectum, to fail, fall short
dēfōrmis, -e, *adj.*, unsightly, degrading
deinde *and* **dein,** *adv.*, thereafter, then
dēlectātio, -ōnis, *f.*, delight, pleasure
dēlectō (1), to attract, delight
dēlicātus, -a, -um, *adj.*, dainty, soft
dēminuō, -ere, -minuī, -minūtum, to diminish, lessen
dēnique, *adv.*, at last, finally
dēnuntiō (1), to announce, declare, threaten
dēpōnō, -ere, -pōsuī, -pōsitum, to put, lay down, put aside
dēpopulor, -ārī, -ātus sum, to depopulate, destroy
dēposcō, -ere, -poposcī, —, to demand, ask for
dēpugnō (1), to fight hard, fight it out
dērīvō (1), to divert
dēsertus, -a, -um, *adj.*, abandoned, deserted
dēsīderium, -ī, *n.*, desire, longing, grief for absence *or* loss
dēsīderō (1), to long for, miss
dēsidia, -ae, *f.*, idleness, inactivity
dēsiliō, -ere, -siluī, -sultum, to jump down
dēsinō, -ere, -siī, -situm, to cease
dēspērātio, -ōnis, *f.*, hopelessness, despair
dēsum, -esse, -fuī, —,+ *dat.*, to fail, be wanting, be lacking
dētrahō, -ere, -traxī, -tractum, to drag down
dētrīmentum, -ī, *n.*, loss, damage, injury, detriment
deus, -ī, *m.*, god
dīcō, -ere, -dixī, dictum, to say, speak
dictātor, -ōris, *m.*, a chief magistrate
dictitō (1), to say often, assert repeatedly
diēs, diēī, *m.*, day
difficilis, -e, *adj.*, difficult
difficultās, -ātis, *f.*, difficulty, need; obstinacy
dignitās, -ātis, *f.*, worth, merit, esteem, reputation
dignus, -a, -um, *adj.*, deserving, worthy
dīlacerō (1), to tear in pieces
dīlectus, -ūs, *m.*, a recruiting of troops, conscription; a choosing, choice, selection
dīligens, -entis, *adj.*, careful, accurate, diligent
dīligenter, *adv.*, diligently, carefully
dīligentīa, -ae, *f.*, carefulness, diligence, attentiveness
dīligō, -ere, -lexī, -lectum, to love, esteem
dīmicātio, -ōnis, *f.*, a fight, struggle

dīmidium, -ī, *n.*, a half
dīmittō, -ere, -mīsī, -missum, to let go, send away from oneself
dīreptio, -ōnis, *f.*, a plundering, pillaging
discēdō, -ere, -cessī, -cessum, to part, depart, go away
discidium, -ī, *n.*, a tearing apart, division
discō, -ere, didicī, —, to learn, get to know
discordia, -ae, *f.*, dissension, discord
discrīmen, -inis, *n.*, that which divides, dividing line
disertus, -a, -um, *adj.*, expressive, skilled in speaking
dissensio, -ōnis, *f.*, disagreement, variance
diū, *adv.*, for a long time
dīvellō, -ere, -vellī, -vulsum, to tear apart
dīvīnus, -a, -um, *adj.*, divine
dīvitiae, -ārum, *f. pl.*, riches, wealth
dō, dare, dedī, datum, to give, grant, cause
doceō, -ēre, -uī, doctum, to teach, instruct
doctrīna, -ae, *f.*, teaching, instruction
doctus, -a, -um, *adj.*, taught, learned
Dolabella, -ae, *m.*, P. Cornelius Dolabella; defended by Cicero in two court cases, he married Cicero's daughter Terentia in 50 BCE, only to divorce her in 46
doleō, -ēre, -uī, -itum, to grieve, suffer, resent
dolor, -ōris, *m.*, pain, grief
domesticus, -a, -um, *adj.*, relating to the home
dominus, -ī, *m.*, master
domus, -ūs, *f.*, house, home
dubitō (1), to doubt, waiver, hesitate
dūcō, -ere, duxī, ductum, to lead
dulcis, -e, *adj.*, sweet, pleasant
dum, *conj.*, as long as, while, until; provided that
duo, -ae, -o, *adj.*, two
dux, ducis, *m.*, leader, general, ruler
Dyrrachium, -ī, *n.*, Dyrrachium, an important port in Illyria, in earlier times called Epidamnus; modern day Durazzo

ē or **ex,** *prep.* + *abl.*, out of, from
ēdūcō, -ere, -duxī, -ductum, to draw out, lead out
efferō, efferre, extulī, ēlātum, to carry out, bring out
efficiō, -ere, -fēcī, -fectum, to make, effect, produce, accomplish, complete
efflōrescō, -ere, -flōruī, —, to blossom, break into bloom
effugiō, -ere, -fūgī, -fugitum, to flee, escape, get off
egens, -entis, *adj.*, needy, destitute; in need of
egeō, -ēre, -uī, to be in need, to want, to be in need of something + *abl.*

egestās, -ātis, *f.*, poverty, indigence
ego, *pron.*, I
ēgregius, -a, -um, *adj.*, admirable, distinguished, extraordinary
ēiciō, -ere, -iēcī, -iectum, to throw out, cast out, reject
ēlabōrō (1), to labor hard, strive
ēlectio, -ōnis, *f.*, choice, selection
ēlocūtio, -ōnis, *f.*, a speaking out, expression, elocution, style
ēloquens, -entis, *adj.*, eloquent
ēloquentia, -ae, *f.*, eloquence
enim, *conj.*, indeed, truly
Ennius, -ī, *m.*, perhaps the greatest of the early Latin poets (239–169 BCE), whose most famous work, *Annales*, a poem written in dactylic hexameters and surviving in fragments, recounted the history of Rome
Ēpīrus, -ī, *f.*, a country in Greece between Macedonia and Thessaly, part of modern day Albania
eques, -itis, *m.*, a horseman, rider; **Equites,** the order of knights
equidem, *adv.*, indeed, truly
equus, -ī, *m.*, a horse
ergō, *adv.*, therefore
ēripiō, -ere, -ripuī, -reptum, to snatch away
error, -ōris, *m.*, error, mistake
ērudiō, -īre, -īvī, -ītum, to instruct, teach, educate
ērudītio, -ōnis, *f.*, teaching, instruction, knowledge
ērudītus, -a, -um, *adj.*, instructed, educated
et, *conj.*, and
etenim, *conj.*, for indeed
etiam, *conj.*, also, even
etiamsi, *conj.*, even if, although
Etrūria, -ae, *f.*, a region of central Italy, modern day Tuscany
ēveniō, -īre, -vēnī, -ventum, to come out
ēvertō, -ere, -vertī, -versum, to overturn, throw down; to turn out
ex *or* **e,** *prep.+ abl.*, from, out of
excēdō, -ere, -cessī, -cessum, to go out, leave
excellens, -tis, *adj.*, high, lofty, eminent, distinguished
excellō, -ere, —, —, to stand out, be distinguished
excipiō, -ere, -cēpī, -ceptum, to receive, take up, catch
excitō (1), to rouse forth, arouse
exclūdō, -ere, -clūsī, -clūsum, to shut out, exclude
excolō, -ere, -coluī, -cultum, to tend or cultivate carefully
exemplar, -āris, *m.*, a copy, likeness
exemplum, -ī, *n.*, example
exeō, -īre, -iī, -itum, to go out
exercitātio, -ōnis, *f.*, practice, exercise

exercitus, -ūs, *m.*, a trained body of soldiers, army; training
exiguus, -a, -um, *adj.*, small, scanty, inadequate, trivial
eximius, -a, -um, *adj.*, exceptional, distinguished; excepted
eximō, -ere, -ēmī, -emptum, to take out, take away
existimō (1), to form a judgment, consider, regard
exitium, -ī, *n.*, destruction, ruin
expedītus, -a, -um, *adj.*, lightly equipped
expetō, -ere, -īvī, -ītum, to desire, strive after
expressus, -a, -um, *adj.*, prominent, distinct
exprōmō, -ere, -prompsī, -promptum, to show, reveal
exsilium, -ī, *n.*, banishment, exile
exsistō, -ere, -stitī, -stitum, to stand forth, come forth, appear
exspectātio, -onis, *f.*, expectation, a waiting for, a looking for
exstinguō, -ere, -stinxī, -stinctum, to put out; to destroy
exterus, -a, -um, *adj.*, foreign
extorqueō, -ēre, -torsī, -tortum, to twist out, wrest away
extrēmus, -a, -um, *adj.*, final, furthest, edge of
facētia, -ae, *f.*, wit, humor
facilis, -e, *adj.*, easy
facinorōsus, -a, -um, *adj.*, wicked, criminal
facinus, -oris, *n.*, crime
faciō, -ere, fēcī, factum, to make, do
factum, -ī, *n.*, a deed, something that has been done
facultās, -ātis, *f.*, capacity, ability; opportunity, means
falsus, -a, -um, *adj.*, untrue, wrong
familia, -ae, *f.*, a household of slaves, household, family; a band of gladiators
fateor, -ērī, fassus sum, to grant, acknowledge, say
faveō, -ēre, fāvī, fautum, + *dat.*, to favor, support
Favōnius, -ī *m.*, Marcus Favonius, an staunch opponent of Clodius, a friend of Cato the Younger, and later one of the assassins of Julius Caesar
Februārius, -a, -um, *m.*, belonging to the month of February
fēlīcitās, -ātis, *f.*, good fortune, success
fēmina, -ae, *f.*, female, a woman
ferē, *adv.*, nearly, almost
ferō, ferre, tulī, lātum, to carry, bring, bear, endure
festīnō (1), to hurry, hasten
fēstus, -a, -um, *adj.*, of a holiday, festive

fidēlis, -e, *adj.*, faithful
fidēs, -ēī, *f.*, trust, faith, loyalty
fiō, fierī, factus sum, to be made, come into existence; to happen, become
firmitās, -ātis, *f.*, firmness, stability, constancy
firmus, -a, -um, *adj.*, firm, strong
flāmen, -inis, *m.*, a priest
flētus, -ūs, *m.*, weeping, wailing
flōs, -ōris, *m.*, a flower
fluitō (1), to flow here and there; to float, be tossed about
fons, fontis, *m.*, spring, well, source
forensis, -e, *adj.*, relating to the forum
foris, *adv.*, outside
Formiae, -arum, *f.*, a coastal town in southern Latium, where Cicero had a villa
forsitan, *adv.*, perhaps, perchance
fortasse *adv.*, perhaps
fortis, -e, *adj.*, strong, brave
fortitūdo, -inis, *f.*, strength; bravery, courage
fortūna, -ae, *f.*, fate, fortune, chance
fortūnātē, *adv.*, happily, fortunately
forum, -ī, *n.*, an open square, marketplace
frāter, -tris, *m.*, a brother
fraudātio, -ōnis, *f.*, deceit, fraud
fructus, -ūs, *m.*, fruit; profit, enjoyment
fruor, -ī, fructus sum, + *abl.*, to enjoy
fugiō, -ere, fūgī, —, to flee, take flight
funditus, *adv.*, from the bottom; completely, entirely
fundus, -ī, *m.*, ground; soil, estate
fungor, -ī, functus sum, to perform, execute, undergo
Fūrius, -ī *m.*, L. Furius Philus, consul in 136 BCE, a leading orator of the day, and a close friend of Scipio Africanus
furō, -ere, to rage, rave at
furor, -ōris, *m.*, madness, insanity

gaudeō, -ēre, gāvīsus sum, to enjoy, delight in
genus, -eris, *n.*, class, group; birth
gerō, -ere, gessī, gestum, to wage, conduct
gestus, -ūs, *m.*, the carriage of the body, posture; the studied gestures of an orator
gignō, -ere, genuī, genitum, to beget, bear, bring forth
gladiātor, -ōris, *m.*, a bandit, brigand; gladiator
gladius, -ī, *m.*, sword
glōria, -ae, *f.*, fame, renown, glory
glōriōse, *adv.*, gloriously, boastfully
glōriōsus, -a, -um, *adj.*, famous, glorious, boastful
gradus, -ūs, *m.*, a step, step up

Graecus, -a, -um, *adj.*, Greek
grātia, -ae, *f.*, pleasantness, favor, grace, influence; **grātias agere,** to give thanks
Grattius, -ī *m.*, Grattius, the prosecutor of Archias
grātus, -a, -um, *adj.*, charming, pleasant, agreeable, grateful
gravis, -e, *adj.*, heavy; serious
gravitās, -ātis, *f.*, dignity, seriousness
grex, gregis, *m.*, a herd, flock, drove
gubernāculum, -ī, *n.*, a rudder, helm; direction, management
gubernō (1), to steer, direct, govern

habeō, -ēre, -uī, -itum, to have, hold
habitus, -ūs, *m.*, bearing, appearance
haud, *adv.*, not, hardly
hauriō, -īre, hausī, haustum, to draw, drink up, drain
Hercules, -is, *m.*, Hercules, son of Jupiter and Alcmena; *used as an oath, in the form* **Hercule** *or* **Mehercule**, by Hercules
hic, haec, hoc, *pron.* or *pronominal adj.*, this
hiemps, hiemis, *f.*, winter, storm
hinc, *adv.*, from here; on this side
histrio, -ōnis, *m.*, an actor
homo, -inis, *m.*, a human being, man
honestās, -ātis, *f.*, honor, respectability
honestus, -a, -um, *adj.*, honorable, virtuous
honōs, -ōris, *f.*, honor; public office
hōra, -ae, *f.*, hour
Hortensius, -ī, *m.*, Quintus Hortensius Hortalus (114–50 BCE, consul in 69), the foremost orator in Rome previous to Cicero's entrance into public life
hortor, -ārī, -ātus sum, to exhort, incite, encourage
hostis, -is, *m.*, enemy
hūmānitas, -tātis, *f.*, humanity, kindness, refinement in taste and education, culture
hūmānus, -a, -um, *adj.*, human

iaceō, -ēre, iacuī, —, to lie
iaciō, -ere, iecī, iactum, to throw, cast, hurl
iam, *adv.*, now, already
ibi, *adv.*, there, in that place, in that thing
idcirco, *adv.*, on that account
īdem, eadem, idem, *pron.*, the same
igitur, *adv.*, then, therefore
ignāvia, -ae, *f.*, idleness
ignis, -is, *m.*, fire
ignōrō (1), to be unaware of, not know
ille, illa, illud, *pron.*, that; that well-known
illinc, *adv.*, from that place; on that side

imāgō, -inis, *f.*, image; **imagines,** portrait masks of ancestors; they were displayed in the atria of Roman houses and carried in funeral processions

imbēcillus, -a, -um, *adj.*, weak, feeble

imberbis, -e, *adj.*, beardless

imitor, -ārī, -ātus sum, to imitate, copy

immo, *particle,* on the contrary, indeed

immortālis, -e, *adj.*, deathless, immortal

impedīmenta, -ōrum, *n. pl.*, baggage

impediō, -īre, -pedīvī, -pedītum, to entangle, ensnare

impendeō, -ēre, -pependī, —, to hang over, threaten

imperātor, -ōris, *m.*, a commander, leader

imperō (1), to order

impetus, -ūs, *m.*, attack, impulse

improbus, -a, -um, *adj.*, bad, wicked, depraved

impudīcus, -a, -um, *adj.*, shameless

impūrus, -a, -um, *adj.*, impure, vile, infamous

in, *prep.+ abl.*, in, on; + *acc.*, into, onto, towards, against

inānis, -e, *adj.*, empty, vain

inaugurō (1), to consecrate, install

incertus, -a, -um, *adj.*, uncertain

incidō, -ere, -cidī, -cāsum, to fall upon; to happen

incipiō, -ere, -cēpī, -ceptum, to begin

incitō (1), to stir up, urge on, rouse, incite

incommodus, -a, -um, *adj.*, inconvenient, troublesome, disagreeable

incrēdibilis, -e, *adj.*, not to be believed, incredible

incurrō, -ere, -currī, -cursum, to run into; to attack

indicō (1), to show, indicate

indignus, -a, -um, *adj.*, unworthy

industria, -ae, *f.*, industry, diligence

inertia, -ae, *f.*, slothfulness

infīnītus, -a, -um, *adj.*, infinite, unbounded

ingenium, -ī, *n.*, nature, natural ability; mental power, cleverness, talent,

ingrātus, -a, -um, *adj.*, ungrateful, unpleasant, unpleasing

inhūmānus, -a, -um, *adj.*, inhuman, cruel, rude, uncultivated

inimīcus, -a, -um, *adj.*, unfriendly, hostile

inīquitās, -tātis, *f.*, unevenness, difficulty, injustice

inīquuus, -a, -um, *adj.*, uneven, unfair, inimical

inlustris, -e, *adj.*, full of light, bright, brilliant; distinguished, famous

innumerābilis, -e, *adj.*, innumerable, unable to be counted
inopia, -ae, *f.*, need, poverty
inquam, *defective verb*, I say
inrīdeō, -ēre, -rīsī, -rīsum, to laugh at, mock
inrīsio. *See* **irrīsio**
insidiae, -ārum, *f. pl.*, an ambush, trap
insidiator, -ōris, *m.*, waylayer, lurker
instituō, -ere, -uī, -ūtum, to put in place, draw up in order
instruō, -ere, -struxī, -structum, to set up, prepare
insum, inesse, infuī, to be in, to be present in
integer, -gra, -grum, *adj.*, complete, whole, entire
integritās, -ātis, *f.*, soundness, health; uprightness, purity
intellegō, -ere, -lexī, -lectum, to distinguish, perceive
intempestīvus, -a, -um, *adj.*, unseasonable, untimely
inter, *prep.+ acc.*, among, between
intereō, -īre, -iī, -itum, to be lost from among, perish
interficiō, -ere, -fēcī, -fectum, to kill, slay
interim, *adv.*, meanwhile
interpōnō, -ere, -posuī, -positum, to put between or among
interpretor, -ārī, —, to understand in a certain sense
intersum, -esse, -fuī, to be between, to be present, take part in; *impers.*, **interest,** it concerns, it is of importance
intueor, -ērī, -tuitus sum, to look at attentively, gaze at, consider
inūtilis, -e, *adj.*, useless, unprofitable
invehō, -ere, -vexī, -vectum, to carry in, convey
inveniō, -īre, -vēnī, -ventum, to find
invideō, -ēre, -vīdī, -vīsum, to look upon with the evil eye; to envy, begrudge
invītus, -a, -um, *adj.*, unwilling
iocōsus, -a, -um, *adj.*, humorous, merry
ipse, -a, -um, *adj.*, he (*emphatic*) himself, herself, itself
īra, -ae, *f.*, anger, rage
īrācundia, -ae, *f.*, state of anger
īrātus, -a, -um, *adj.*, angry
irrīsio, -ōnis, *f.*, mocking, derision
is, ea, id, *pron.*, he, she, it; this, that
iste, ista, istud, *pron.*, that
ita, *adv.*, so, thus
Ītalia, -ae, *f.*, Italy
itaque, *adv.*, and so, therefore
item, *adv.*, likewise, also, in like manner
iter, itineris, *n.*, course, journey
iubeō, -ēre, iussī, iussum, to order, command; to ask

iūcundus, -a, -um, *adj.*, pleasant, delightful
iūdex, -icis, *m.*, judge
iūdicium, -ī, *n.*, judgment, a trial; a law court
iūdicō (1), to judge
iunctio, -ōnis, *f.*, a connection, a joining
iungō, -ere, iūnxī, iūnctum, to join
iūrō (1), to swear, take an oath
iūs, iūris, *n.*, broth, soup
iūs, iūris, *n.*, justice, law, right, power, legality
iuvō, -āre, iūvī, iūtum, to help, assist

Kalendae, -ārum, *f. pl.*, the first day of the Roman month

labor, -ōris, *m.*, work, toil, struggle
labōrō (1), to work, strive
labrum, -ī, *n.*, a wash basin, tub, bath
lacessō, -ere, -īvī, -ītum, to provoke, stimulate, excite
lacrima, -ae, *f.*, a tear
Laelius, -ī, *m.*, Gaius Laelius, consul in 140 BCE and intimate friend of Scipio Africanus
Lānuvinus, -a, -um, *adj.*, of or belonging to Lanuvium
Lānuvium, -ī, *n.*, a town in Latium
Latiar, -āris, *n.*, a feast of Jupiter Latiaris
Latīnus, -a, -um, *adj.*, Latin
latro, -ōnis, *m.*, a bandit, brigand, hired servant
latrōcinium, -ī, *n.*, highway robbery, brigandage
laudābilis, -e, *adj.*, praiseworthy, laudable
laudō (1), to praise
laus, laudis, *f.*, praise
lēgitimus, -a, -um, *adj.*, legal
lēnis, -e, *adj.*, smooth, gentle
Lentulus, -ī, *m.*, Publius Cornelius Lentulus Spinther, the consul-elect in 58 BCE
lepidus, -a, -um, *adj.*, pleasant, charming, neat
lepos, -ōris, *m.*, pleasantness, charm, wit
Lepta, -ae, *f.*, Quintus Paconius Lepta, who served as Cicero's *praefectus fabrum* ("chief engineer" who generally functioned as adjutant to the commander) in Cilicia
Leucas, -adis, *f.*, Leucas, an island off the coast of western Greece, in the Ionian Sea
levis, -e, *adj.*, light
lex, lēgis, *f.*, law
līber, -era, -erum, *adj.*, free, of free birth; **līberī, -ōrum,** children
liber, -brī, *m.*, a book, writing
līberālis, -e, *adj.*, relating to freedom
līberālitās, -ātis, *f.*, courtesy, kindness, generosity
libīdo, -inis, *f.*, violent desire, lust

licet, licuit, *impers.*, it is allowed
Licinius, -ī, *m.*, C. Licinius Macer Calvus, a well-known poet and orator, often mentioned in connection with the circle of the poet Catullus
litterae, -ārum, *f. pl.*, letter, written records, documents
locus, -ī, *m.*, place, position
loquor, -ī, locūtus sum, to speak, talk, say
luctus, -ūs, *m.*, mourning, lamentation, grieving
lūdus, -ī, *m.*, play, game, sport; public games
lūgeō, -ēre, luxī, luctum, to grieve, mourn
lūmen, -inis, *n.*, light; eye
lux, lūcis, *f.*, light, day
luxuria, -ae, *f.*, excess, extravagance
Lyso, -ōnis, *m.*, Cicero's host in Patrae

Macer, -crī, *m.*, C. Licinius Macer Calvus, a well-known poet and orator, often mentioned in connection with the circle of the poet Catullus
magis, *adv.*, more
magister, -trī, *f.*, a teacher; master, chief
magnificentia, -ae, *f.*, loftiness, grandeur
magnitūdo, -inis, *f.*, greatness
magnus, -a, -um, *adj.*, great, big
maledicē, *adv.*, abusively
mālō, malle, māluī, —, to prefer, wish rather, choose rather
malus, -a, -um, *adj.*, bad, evil
mancus, -a, -um, *adj.*, imperfect, defective; crippled
maneō, -ēre, mansī, mansum, to stay, remain
manicātus, -a, -um, *adj.*, having long sleeves
manus, -ūs, *f.*, a hand; band of men
Martius, -a, -um, *adj.*, relating to the god Mars; relating to the month of March
mātūrē, *adv.*, at the right time, opportunely; soon, too soon, early
mātūritās, -ātis, *f.*, ripeness, development
medicīna, -ae, *f.*, medicine, remedy
medicus, -ī, *m.*, doctor, physician
mediocris, -e, *adj.*, moderate, ordinary
memoria, -ae, *f.*, memory, the capacity for remembering
mens, mentis, *f.*, mind, thought
mensis, -is, *m.*, a month
Mescinius, -ī, *m.*, Lucius Mescinius Rufus, who served as Cicero's quaestor while in Cilicia
mētior, -īrī, mentus sum, to measure, estimate, judge

meus, -a, -um, *adj.*, my, mine
mīles, -itis, *m.*, soldier
Milō, -ōnis, *m.*, T. Annius Milo Papianus, tribune who worked for Cicero's recall from exile in 57 BCE; subsequently defended by Cicero when on trial for the murder of Clodius, whom he killed in a scuffle on the Appian Way in 52
Minerva, -ae, *f.*, Minerva, daughter of Jupiter, goddess of wisdom
minimē, *adv.*, not at all, by no means
minitor, -ārī, -ātus sum, to threaten
minor, -ārī, -ātus sum, to threaten
mīror, -ārī, -ātus sum, to marvel, be amazed at
misceō, -ēre, miscuī, mixtum, to mix, mingle, combine
miser, -era, -erum, *adj.*, wretched, poor
misericordia, -ae, *f.*, compassion, pity
mittō, -ere, mīsī, missum, to send, let go, pass over
moderātio, -ōnis, *f.*, moderation, restraint, temperance
moderātus, -a, -um, *adj.*, restrained, controlled
moderō (1), to regulate, moderate, restrain
modicē, *adv.*, moderately
modo, *adv.*, only, merely, just
modus, -ī, *m.*, way, manner; limit
molestia, -ae, *f.*, annoyance, trouble
molestus, -a, -um, *adj.*, burdensome, troublesome, annoying
moneō, -ēre, monuī, monītum, to warn, advise
monumentum, -ī, *n.*, memorial; written memorials, annals
mōrātus, -a, -um, *adj.*, endowed with a character or manners of a certain kind
moror, -ārī, morātus sum, to delay, linger
mōrōsus, -a, -um, *adj.*, morose, peevish, obstinate
mors, -tis, *f.*, death
mortuus, -a, -um, *adj.*, dead
mōs, mōris, *m.*, custom, habit; *pl.*, character
motus, -ūs, *m.*, movement, upheaval
moveō, -ēre, mōvī, mōtum, to move, set in motion, excite, arouse
muliēbris, -e, *adj.*, womanly, feminine, unmanly
mulier, -eris, *f.*, a woman
muliercula, -ae, *f.*, a little woman
multitūdo, -inis, *f.*, a large number, multitude
multum, *adv.*, much, very
multus, -a, -um, *adj.*, much, many
mūnicipium, -ī, *n.*, a town

mūnus, -eris, *n.*, an office, function, duty; public office
mūtō (1), to change
mūtuus, -a, -um, *adj.*, mutual, reciprocal

nam, *conj.*, for, because
nascor, -ī, nātus sum, to be born
nātio, -ōnis, *f.*, a tribe, race, people
nātūra, -ae, *f.*, nature
nātus, -ī, *m.*, a son
naufragus, -ī, *m.*, a shipwrecked person
nāvigātio, -ōnis, *f.*, a voyage, a sailing
nāvigō (1), to sail, voyage
nāvis, -is, *f.*, a ship, vessel
nē, *conj.*, lest, so that not
-ne, *particle, indicating a question*
nec, neque, *conj.*, nor, and not
necessārius, -a, -um, *adj.*, necessary
necessārius, -ī, *m.*, a close friend
necesse, *indecl. adj., n.*, necessary, unavoidable, fated (only with *esse* and *habere*)
neglegō, -ere, -lexī, -lectum, to neglect, disregard
negō (1), to deny, say. . . not
negōtium, -ī, *n.*, business
nēmo, -inis, *m.*, no man, no one, nobody
nesciō, -īre, -īvī, —, to not know
nihil, *n. indecl.*, nothing
nīmīrum, *adv.*, undoubtedly, truly, certainly
nimius, -a, -um, *adj.*, too much, too great, excessive
nisi, *conj.*, unless, except, if not
nitidus, -a, -um, *adj.*, bright, shining
nix, nivis, *f.*, snow
nōbilis, -e, *adj.*, noble, renowned
nōmen, -inis, *n.*, a name
nōminō (1), to name, give a name to
nōn, *adv.*, not
Nōnae, -ārum, *f.*, the nones, the ninth day before the Ides; thus the fifth day of all months except March, May, July, October, when it was on the seventh
nonne, *interr. adv., asks a question to which an affirmative answer is expected*
nōs, pl. of **ego**, we
noster, -stra, -strum, *adj.*, our
November, -bris, -bre, belonging to the month of November
novus, -a, -um, *adj.*, new, recent
nox, noctis, *f.*, night
nūdus, -a, -um, *adj.*, naked, bare
nullus, -a, -um, *adj.*, no, none
num, *interr. particle, asks a question to which a negative answer is expected*
numerō (1), to count

numerus, -ī, *m.*, a measure, number
numquam (or **nunquam**), *adv.*, never
nunc, *adv.*, now
nūper, *adv.*, recently, lately, not long ago
nusquam, *adv.*, nowhere

ō! *interjection,* oh!
ob, *prep.+ acc.*, because of, on account of; in front of, before
obeō, -īre, -īvī, -itum, to go to *or* over
ōbiciō, -ere, -iēcī, -iectum, to throw in the way
obiurgātio, -ōnis, *f.*, a blaming, reproving
obiurgō (1), to scold, reprove
oblectō (1), to attract; to please, amuse
obscūrus, -a, -um, *adj.*, obscure, hidden
obsēcrō (1), to beg, beseech earnestly, pray
obstō, -āre, -stetī, —, to obstruct, stand in the way
obsum, obesse, obfuī, —, to be in the way, be against
obtemperō (1), to submit to, obey, comply with
obtrectātor, -ōris, *m.*, a disparager
obviam, *adv.*, in the way, on the way; *hence,* **obviam fieri** + *dat.*, to meet
occīdō, -ere, -cīdī, -cīsum, to kill
occurrō, -ere, -currī, -cursum, to work against, oppose; to run to meet
Octōber, -bris, -bre, belonging to the month of October, the eighth month of the Roman year
ōdī, ōdisse, to hate, detest
odium, -ī, *n.*, hatred
offendō, -ere, -fendī, -fensum, to strike against, offend, displease
officiōsus, -a, -um, *adj.*, attentive, courteous, dutiful, obliging
officium, -ī, *n.*, dutiful action, duty; political office
omittō, -mittere, -mīsī, -missum, to let go, let fall
omnīnō, *adv.*, altogether, entirely, wholly
omnis, -e, *adj.*, every, all
opera, -ae, *f.*, work, effort, support; **operam dare,** to work hard at
opes, opum, *f. pl.*, riches, wealth
opīnio, -ōnis, *f.*, opinion
opīnor, -ārī, -ātus sum, to be of opinion, believe, suppose
oportet, oportēre, oportuit, *impers. verb,* it is proper, one ought to
oppetō, -ere, -īvī, -ītum, to encounter, go to meet; to die
oppidum, -ī, *n.*, a town
oppōnō, -ere, -posuī, -positum, to place before; to oppose
opportūnitās, -ātis, *f.*, convenience, advantage

opportūnus, -a, -um, *adj.*, opportune, fit, suitable
opprimō, -ere, -pressī, -pressum, to press upon, press down, crush
oppugnō (1), to attack, assault
optemperō. *See* **obtemperō**
opus, -eris, *n.*, work, task
ōrātio, -ōnis, *f.*, speaking, speech, language
ōrātor, -ōris, *m.*, a speaker, orator
orbō (1), to bereave, deprive of
ornāmentum, -ī, *n.*, equipment, embellishment, ornament
ornō (1), to equip, furnish, fit out
ōs, ōris, *n.*, the mouth; face
ostendō, -ere, -tendī, -tentum, to hold out, show, display
ōtium, -ī, *n.*, free time, leisure; peace

pactum, -ī, *n.*, a way; an agreement, pact
paene, *adv.*, nearly, almost
paenula, -ae, *f.*, a travelling cloak
paenulātus, -a, -um, *adj.*, clothed in a traveler's cloak
pāgina, -ae, *f.*, a leaf or page of paper, *or* of a book; tablet
palam, *adv.*, openly, publicly
parātus, -a, -um, *adj.*, prepared, ready
parcō, -ere, pepercī, parsum, to spare, be frugal with (+ *dat.*)
parens, -entis, *m.* and *f.*, parent
pariō, -ere, peperī, partum, to bring forth, bear
parricīda, -ae, *m.*, a parricide
pars, partis, *f.*, part
partim, *adv.*, partly, some
partiō, -īre, partīvī, partītus, to share out, distribute, divide
parum, *adv.*, too little
parvus, -a, -um, *adj.*, small, little
pater, -tris, *m.*, father; senator
patior, patī, passus sum, to suffer, endure, allow
patria, -ae, *f.*, fatherland, native land
patrius, -a, -um, *adj.*, ancestral
patrōcinium, -ī, *n.*, defense, protection
paucitās, -ātis, *f.*, fewness, scarcity, paucity
paucus, -a, -um, *usually in the pl.*, **paucī, -ae, -a,** *adj.*, few, little
paulisper, *adv.*, for a little while
paulus, -a, -um, *adj.*, little, small; **paulo,** by a little
Paulus, -ī, *m.*, name of the family of the *gens Aemilia*; L. Aemilius Paulus, consul in 50 BCE
pax, pācis, *f.*, peace
pecūnia, -ae, *f.*, property, money
pellō, -ere, pepulī, pulsum, to drive away
penātēs, -ium, *m. pl.*, household gods

penitus, *adv.*, deeply
pēnūria, -ae, *f.*, lack, want
per, *prep.+ acc.*, through, along, during, by means of, for, by
percipiō, -ere, -cēpī, -ceptum, to lay hold of, seize; to receive mentally, learn, comprehend
perdō, -ere, -didī, -ditum, to lose, destroy
peregrīnor, -ārī, peregrīnus sum, to wander, ramble
peregrīnus, -ī, *m.*, a foreigner, stranger
pereō, -īre, -iī, -itum, to die, perish, be ruined
perfectus, -a, -um, *adj.*, perfect, complete, finished
perferō, -ferre, -tulī, -lātum, to bear, endure; carry through
perfruor, -ī, perfructus sum, to enjoy fully
perfugium, -ī, *n.*, a place of refuge, shelter
perfungor, -ī, perfunctus sum, to go through, endure
perīculum, -ī, *n.*, a trial, test; danger, peril
permagnus, -a, -um, *adj.*, very great, very large
permaneō, -ēre, -mansī, -mansum, to endure, last
perniciōsus, -a, -um, *adj.*, destructive, ruinous
pernoctō (1), to pass the night
pernoscō, -ere, -nōvī, -nōtum, to investigate thoroughly, become thoroughly acquainted with
perpetuus, -a, -um, *adj.*, continuous
persequor, -ī, -secūtus sum, to pursue, follow after
perspiciō, -ere, -spexī, -spectum, to see through, look through
pertimescō, -ere, -timuī, —, to become very much afraid of
pertinax, -ācis, *adj.*, tenacious, stubborn
perturbātio, -ōnis, *f.*, disorder, disturbance
perturbātus, -a, -um, *adj.*, disturbed, confused
perversitas, -ātis, *f.*, perversity
pestilentia, -ae, *f.*, pestilence, plague, infectious disease
petītio, -ōnis, *f.*, a standing for office, candidature
petō, -ere, -īvī, -ītum, to seek, ask, make for, aim at
petulans, -antis, *adj.*, impudent, capricious, petulant, wanton
petulantia, -ae, *f.*, impudence
pexus, -a, -um, *adj.*, combed
Philotimus, -ī, *m.*, Philotimus, Terentia's freedman, who often assisted Cicero with financial and domestic affairs
pietās, -ātis, *f.*, dutiful behavior, devotion
pigritia, -ae, *f.*, sluggishness, indolence
pila, -ae, *f.*, a ball
pinguis, -e, *adj.*, fat, fertile

Pīso, -ōnis, *m.,* a name of the *gens Calpurnia;* L. Calpurnius Piso Caesoninus, consul in 58 BCE; C. Calpurnius Piso Frugi, the son-in-law of Cicero

placeō, -ēre, -uī, -ītum, to please, be acceptable, agreeable

Plancius, -ī, *m.,* Gnaeus Plancius, Quaestor in Macedonia in 58 BCE, provided aid and protection to Cicero while in exile

plānē, *adv.,* plainly, quite, thoroughly

plaudō, -ere, plausī, plausum, to clap, strike, applaud

plēnus, -a, -um, *adj.,* full

plērique, -raeque, -raque, very many, a great part, the majority

plērumque, *adv.,* for the most part, generally

plūs, plūris, *adj.,* more

poēta, -ae, *m.,* a poet

Pompeius, -ī, *m.,* Gnaeus Pompeius Magnus (Pompey the Great), triumvir with Crassus and Caesar, defeated by Caesar in the Civil War and subsequently killed in Egypt

pōnō, -ere, posuī, positum, to put, place

populus, -ī, *m.,* people, race

porro, *adv.,* forward, further, next

portus, -ūs, *m.,* haven, refuge

possessio, -ōnis, *f.,* possession; occupation, enjoyment

possum, posse, potuī, —, to be able

post, *adv.,* behind, after

post, *prep. + acc.,* behind, after

postērus, -a, -um, *adj.,* subsequent, following, next, future

postrēmus, -a, -um, *adj.,* last, final

postrīdiē, *adv.,* on the next day, the day after

potentia, -ae, *f.,* power, might, ability

potior, -us, *adj.,* preferable, better

potissimum, *adv.,* chiefly, above all

praebeō, -ēre, -buī, -bitum, to offer, show, provide

praeceptum, -ī, *n.,* a precept, rule, command

praecipiō, -ere, -cēpī, -ceptum, to take before, receive in advance; to instruct, teach

praeclārus, -a, -um, *adj.,* very bright, remarkable, distinguished; *in a bad sense,* notorious

praedicō (1), to proclaim, declare

praedium, -ī, *n.,* a plot of land, a landed estate

praedo, -ōnis, *m.,* a robber, plunderer; pirate

praelūceō, -ēre, -luxī, —, to shine, carry a light before

praemium, -ī, *n.*, the first pick; a gift, award
praepōnō, -ere, -posuī, -positum, to put before, place before, prefer
praesens, -entis, *adj.*, present, at hand
praesertim, *adv.*, especially, chiefly
praesidium, -ī, *n.*, a protection, defense
praestans, -antis, *adj.*, outstanding, distinguished, excellent
praestō, *adv.*, present, at hand, here, ready
praestō, -stāre, -stitī, -stitum, to stand before, be distinguished; to show, present
praeter, *adv.*, except
praetereā, *adv.*, besides, beyond this, further
praetōrius, -a, -um, *adj.*, relating to the praetor, praetorian
praetūra, -ae, *f.*, the office of praetor at Rome; eight were elected annually; they played an important role in civil procedures and presided over a several of the criminal courts
premō, -ere, pressī, pressum, to press, press upon
prīdiē, *adv.*, on the day before
prīmum, *adv.*, first
prīmus, -a, -um, *adj.*, first, foremost
principium, -ī, *n.*, a beginning, origin
prīvatus, -ī, *m.*, a private person; someone who holds no public office
pro, *prep.+ abl.*, before, in front of; for, on behalf of
probitas, -ātis, *f.*, probity, uprightness, honesty
prōbō (1), to approve, prove, test
procul, *adv.*, far from
prōdeō, -īre, -iī, -itum, to advance, go forward; to come out, appear, show itself
prōdūcō, -ere, -duxī, -ductum, to lead forth; to bring before a court or assembly
proelium, -ī, *n.*, battle, fight
profecto, *adv.*, truly, really, indeed
prōferō, -ferre, -tulī, -lātum, to bring forth
prōficiscor, -ficiscī, -fectus sum, to start forward, set out
prōflīgātus, -a, -um, *adj.*, ruined, degraded
profundum, -ī, *n.*, depth, abyss; the sea
prohibeō, -ēre, -uī, -itum, to restrain, hinder
prope, *adv.*, near
propinquitās, -ātis, *f.*, nearness; friendship
propinquus, -a, -um, *adj.*, near, neighboring
prōpōnō, -ere, -posuī, -positum, to put forth, display

proprius, -a, -um, *adj.*, one's own, particular
propter, *prep.+ acc.*, near; on account of
prōpugnāculum, -ī, *n.*, fortress, defense, fortification
prōpugnō (1), to fight in defense, defend
proscriptio, -ōnis, *f.*, a proscription
prōsequor, -sequī, -secūtus sum, to follow, accompany
prosperus, -a, -um, *adj.*, fortunate, successful
prosum, prodesse, profuī, —, + *dat.*, to benefit, profit
prōvideō, -vidēre, -vīsī, -vīsum, to look forward, foresee; to provide for
prōvincia, -ae, *f.*, a province
prōvinciālis, -e, *adj.*, of or relating to a province
proximus, -a, -um, *adj.*, the nearest, next
prūdentia, -ae, *f.*, prudence, discretion
pruīna, -ae, *f.*, hoar-frost, rime; cold, winter
publicus, -a, -um, *adj.*, belonging to the people, public
pudeō, -ēre, -uī, -itum, to be ashamed; *often as an impers. verb,* **pudet, puduit,** it causes shame, one feels ashamed
pudīcitia, -ae, *f.*, modesty, virtue
pudor, -ōris, *m.*, sense of shame, modesty, decency
puer, -ī, *m.*, boy
puerīlis, -e, *adj.*, youthful, boyish
pugnō (1), to fight
putō (1), to consider, think,

quā, *adv.*, by which way, where; by what way? how?
quadrīduum, -ī, *n.*, a space of four days
quaerō, -ere, -sīvī, -sītum, to seek, ask, question
quaestor, -ōris, *m.*, a Roman magistrate elected to serve one year; quaestors were primarily financial officers who had charge of the state treasury, or who were attached to senior magistrates in the provinces; their number varied, though during most of Cicero's lifetime, there were twenty
quālis, -e, *adj.*, of what kind; of such a kind, like, as
quam, *adv.*, how; than
quamquam, *conj.*, although, though
quantum, *adv.*, as much as, to as great an extent
quantus, -a, -um, *adj.*, how great
quantuscumque, -acumque, -umcumque, *adj.*, however great
quārē, *rel. adv.*, therefore, on which account
quasi, *adv.*, as if, just as
quātenus, *adv.*, how far, to what extent

-que, *conj.,* and
queō, quīre, quīvī, quitum, to be able
quī, quae, quod, *rel. pron.,* who, what, which?
quia, *rel.,* because
quīdam, quaedam, quoddam, *adj.,* a certain person *or* thing
quidem, *adv.,* indeed, even
quin, *in statements to add emphasis,* rather, but indeed; *in subordinate clauses with subjunctive* (*after a negative*), who not, that not; *after negative verbs of doubting,* but that
quintus, -a, -um, *adj.,* fifth
Quirītēs, -ium, *m. pl.,* originally the name of those living in the town of Cures; after the union of the Romans and the Sabines, it refers to the citizens of Rome acting in their civil capacity
quis, quid? *pron., adj.,* who, what?
quispiam, quaepiam, quodpiam, *adj.,* anyone, anything, someone, something
quisquam, quicquam, *indef. pron.,* anyone, anybody
quisque, quaeque, quidque, *indef. pron.,* each, each one, each person
quō, *adv.,* where
quoad, *adv.,* until
quōcircā, *conj.,* wherefore, on which account
quod, *conj.,* because
quoniam, *conj.,* since, because
quoque, *conj.,* also, too
quōquō, *adv.,* to whatever place
quotienscumque, *adv.,* however often

raeda, -ae, *f.,* a four-wheeled travelling carriage
raedārius, -ī, *m.,* driver of a *raeda*
rapīna, -ae, *f.,* pillage, plundering, robbery
rārō, *adv.,* seldom, rarely
ratio, -ōnis, *f.,* a reckoning, account; reason
recipiō, -ere, -cepī, -ceptum, to take back, regain, recover
recolō, -ere, -coluī, -cultum, to practice again, resume
recordātio, -ōnis, *f.,* a recollection, remembrance
recordor, -ārī, -ātus sum, to remember
recreō (1), to create again, restore to soundness, revive, refresh
rectus, -a, -um, *adj.,* right, correct, proper
recurrō, -ere, -currī, -cursum, to run back, hasten back
redemptor, -ōris, *m.,* a contractor, buyer
redeō, -īre, rediī, reditum, to go back, return
redundō (1), to overflow, stream over, be in excess

referō, referre, rettuli, relatum, to bring back; to ascribe, refer, put down to

rēfert, rēferre, retulit, *impers. verb,* it makes a difference, it is important, it matters

reficiō, -ere, -fēcī, -fectum, to make again, restore

regio, -ōnis, *f.*, region, territory, district, direction/boundary line

reiciō, -ere, -iēcī, -iectum, to throw back, behind

relaxō (1), to loosen, relax

religio, -ōnis, *f.*, respect for what is sacred, religious scruple, awe; moral scruples, conscientiousness

religiōsus, -a, -um, *adj.*, sacred, holy, scrupulous

relinquō, -ere, relīquī, relictum, to leave, abandon

reliquus, -a, -um, *adj.*, remaining

remissio, -ōnis, *f.*, a returning, letting go back; relaxation, recreation

remittō, -ere, -mīsī, -missum, to remit, send back, send again; to relax, concede, forgive

removeō, -ēre, -mōvī, -mōtum, to remove

repellō, -ere, -pulsī, -pulsum, to drive back

reperiō, -īre, repperī, repertum, to find, discover

repetō, -ere, -petīvī, -petītum, to seek again, revert to

reprehendō, -ere, -hendī, -hensum, to catch, hold, seize

repugnō (1), to fight against, oppose, resist

requiēs, -ētis, *f.*, rest, repose

rēs, reī, *f.*, thing, matter, event, affair

rēs publica, reī publicae, *f.*, the Roman Republic

respondeō, -ēre, -spondī, -sponsum, to come up to, answer to

restinguō, -ere, -stinxī, -stinctum, to put out again, extinguish, quench

restō, -stāre, -stitī, —, to make stand against, resist; to remain

retardō (1), to slow down, impede

retineō, -ēre, -tinuī, -tentum, to keep back, restrain

revocō (1), to recall, call back

Rhodus, -ī, *m.*, Rhodes, and island off the southwest coast of Asia Minor

rīdiculum, -ī, *n.*, a joke

rōbur, -oris, *n.*, hard wood, oak; strength

rogō (1), to ask, inquire, question

Rōma, -ae, *f.*, Rome

Rōmānus, -a, -um, *adj.*, Roman

rursus, *adv.*, back, backward, on the contrary, again

rusticor, -ārī, rusticus sum, to live in the country, rusticate

saepe, *adv.,* often
saltō (1), to dance
salus, -ūtis, *f.,* health, soundness
salūtāriter, *adv.,* beneficially, advantageously
salveō, -ēre, to be well, in good health; *usually used in the form of a command, as a greeting,* Greetings!, good day!
salvus, -a, -um, *adj.,* safe, well, sound
sanctus, -a, -um, *adj.,* holy, sacred
sānus, -a, -um, *adj.,* sound, healthy, rational
sapiens, -entis, *m.,* a wise man, a philosopher, a sage
sapientia, -ae, *f.,* wisdom
sapiō, -ere, -īvī *or* **-iī,** to taste; to discern, think, be sensible
satis, *adv.,* enough, sufficiently
saucius, -a, -um, *adj.,* wounded, hurt
scaena, -ae, *f.,* the stage, the theatre
scelus, -eris, *n.,* crime, evil deed
scientia, -ae, *f.,* a knowing, knowledge of
sciō, -īre, -īvī, -ītum, to know, know how to
Scīpio, -ōnis, *m.,* a family of the *gens Cornelia,* one of the most eminent members of which was Publius Scipio Africanus Minor, the conqueror of Carthage in 146 BCE, prominent statesman, and influential man of letters
scortum, -ī, *n.,* a harlot, prostitute
scrībō, -ere, scripsī, scriptum, to write, draw
scriptor, -ōris, *m.,* a writer, author
secō, -āre, -uī, -ctum, to cut, cut off
secundus, -a, -um, *adj.,* following, favorable
secus, *adv.,* otherwise
sed, *conj.,* but
sēdēs, -is, *m.,* seat, abode, home
sēditio, -ōnis, *f.,* a going apart, sedition, dissension, quarrel
sēdō (1), to settle, soothe, calm
sēminārium, -ī, *n.,* a plantation, nursery
semper, *adv.,* always
senātus, -ūs, *m.,* the Senate
senectus, -ūtis, *f.,* old age
senex, senis, *m.,* old man
sententia, -ae, *f.,* a way of thinking, opinion, thought; vote
sentiō, -īre, sensī, sensum, to feel, realize
sequor, -ī, secūtus sum, to follow, pursue
sērius, -a, -um, *adj.,* serious
sermo, -ōnis, *m.,* talk, conversation, discourse
servus, -ī, *m.,* a slave
Sestius, -ī, *m.,* the name of a Roman *gens;* Publius Sestius, tribune of the people, who worked for Cicero's recall from exile and was subsequently defended by Cicero when he was indicted on a charge of violence (*vis*)

sevēritās, -ātis, *f.*, gravity, seriousness
sevērus, -a, -um, *adj.*, grave, stern
sī, *conj.*, if
sīc, *adv.*, thus, in this way, so
sīca, -ae, *f.*, a dagger
sīcārius, -ī, *m.*, an assassin, murderer
significō (1), to indicate, show
silva, -ae, *f.*, wood, forest
silvestris, -e, *adj.*, wooded
similiter, *adv.*, in like manner
simul, *adv.*, at the same time
sīn, *conj.*, but if, if however
sine, *prep.+ abl.*, without
singulāris, -e, *adj.*, alone, single, individual
singulī, -ae, -a, *adj.*, single, individual
sinus, -ūs, *m.*, bosom, lap
societās, -ātis, *f.*, partnership, companionship; alliance
socius, -ī, *m.*, companion, ally, associate
Sōcraticī, -ōrum, *m. pl.*, followers of Socrates
sōlācium, -ī, *n.*, consolation
soleō, -ēre, solitus sum, to be accustomed
sollemnis, -e, *adj.*, yearly; religious
sōlus, -a, -um, *adj.*, only, sole
somnus, -ī, *m.*, sleep
spargō, -ere, sparsī, sparsum, to sprinkle, scatter
spectō (1), to look at, observe
spēro (1), to hope, hope for
spēs, -eī, *f.*, hope
splendidus, -a, -um, *adj.*, shining, clear, brilliant, splendid
spoliō (1), to plunder, strip
stabilis, -e, *adj.*, firm, steady, stable
statim, *adv.*, immediately
statuō, -ere, -uī, -ūtum, to cause to stand, establish; to decide
status, -ūs, *m.*, a position, state
stō, stāre, stetī, statum, to stand
strēnuē, *adv.*, vigorously, promptly, actively
strepitus, -ūs, *m.*, a loud noise
studiōsus, -a, -um, *adj.*, eager, diligent
studium, -ī, *n.*, zeal, eagerness, striving
stultus, -a, -um, *adj.*, foolish, silly
stuprum, -ī, *n.*, disgrace, defilement
suādeō, -ēre, suāsī, suāsum, to present in a pleasing manner, recommend, persuade
suāvis, -e, *adj.*, sweet, delightful, pleasant, agreeable
subeō, -īre, -iī, -itum, to go under, enter
subitō, *adv.*, suddenly
subsellium, -ī, *n.*, a bench, a bench in a lawcourt
subtīlis, -e, *adj.*, slender, fine; finely woven
succurrō, -ere, -currī, -cursum, to run beneath; to hasten to assist

suffrāgium, -ī, *n.*, vote
sum, esse, fuī, —, to be
summus, -a, -um, *adj.*, very high, highest, greatest, last
sūmō, -ere, sumpsī, sumptum, to take, take up
sumptus, -ūs, *m.*, cost, expense
superō (1), to go over, rise above, surmount, defeat, cross
superus, -a, -um, *adj.*, situated above, upper, higher
suppeditō (1), to provide, supply
suppetō, -ere, -īvī, -ītum, to be in store, be at hand
suprā, *adv.*, above, on top, over; *prep.* + *acc.*, above, over
surgō, -ere, surrexī, surrectum, to rise up, get up, stand
suscenseō, -ēre, -uī, —, + *dat.*, to be angry, bear a grudge
suscipiō, -ere, -cēpī, -ceptum, to take up, support, raise
suspīcio, -ōnis, *f.*, mistrust, suspicion
sustineō, -ēre, -tinuī, -tentum, to support, sustain
suus, -a, -um, *adj.*, his, her, its, their [own]

tabellārius, -ī, *m.*, a letter carrier
tālāris, -e, *adj.*, stretching to the ankles
tālis, -e, *adj.*, such, of such a kind
tam, *adv.*, so, so much
tamen, *adv.*, however, nevertheless
tamquam, *adv.*, so as, just as, like as
tandem, *adv.*, finally, at last
tantus, -a, -um, *adj.*, so great, so much
tēlum, -ī, *n.*, weapon, spear
temeritās, -ātis, *f.*, rashness
temperantia, -ae, *f.*, temperance, moderation
tempestās, -ātis, *f.*, a storm, tempest; period of time, season
tempestīvus, -a, -um, *adj.*, happening at the right time, opportune
templum, -ī, *n.*, temple, precinct
tempus, -oris, *n.*, time; occasion
tenebrae, -ārum, *f. pl.*, darkness, shadows
teneō, -ēre, tenuī, —, to hold, keep, occupy
Terentia, -ae, *f.*, Terentia, Cicero's wife from approximately 80–46 BCE
tergum, -ī, *n.*, back
testis, -is, *m.* or *f.*, one who gives testimony, a witness
testor, -ārī, -ātus sum, to attest, be a witness, give evidence of
theātrum, -ī, *n.*, theater
thēsaurus, -ī, *m.*, a treasure, store, hoard
timor, -ōris, *m.*, fear
Tīro, -ōnis, *m.*, Tiro, Cicero's slave, freed in 53 BCE, who became a close friend and a trusted literary assistant

toga, -ae, *f.*, toga
tolerō (1), to endure, sustain; to carry
tollō, -ere, sustulī, sublātum, to lift, raise, remove, destroy
tot, *adj.*, so many
tōtus, -a, -um, *adj.*, whole, entire
tractō (1), to drag along, manage
trādō, -ere, -didī, -ditum, to hand over, give up, surrender
trahō, -ere, traxī, tractum, to draw, drag
transferō, -ferre, -tulī, -lātum, to carry over, transfer, convey
tribuō, -ere, -uī, -ūtum, to divide out, allot, assign
tribus, -ūs, *f.*, a tribe, a division of the Roman people, based mainly on locality; there were thirty-five in Cicero's time
trīduum, -ī, *n.*, a space of three days
tristis, -e, *adj.*, sorrowful, grim
tū, *pron.*, you
Tullia, -ae, *f.*, Tullia, Cicero's daughter; she died in February 45 BCE
Tulliola, -ae, *f.*, diminutive form of Tullia, Cicero's affectionate nickname for his daughter
tum, *adv.*, then, next
tumulus, -ī, *m.*, a mound of earth, hill
tunica, -ae, *f.*, a sleeved garment, tunic
turbulentus, -a, -um, *adj.*, disturbed, confused, restless
turpitūdo, -inis, *f.*, ugliness; disgrace
Tusculānus, -a, -um, *adj.*, Tusculan, referring to Tusculum, a town in Latium near modern Frascati where Cicero had a villa
tūtō, *adv.*, safely
tūtus, -a, -um, *adj.*, safe, secure
tuus, -a, -um, *adj.*, your (sing.)
Tyrannio, -ōnis, *m.*, a nickname for Theophrastus of Amisus, a renowned scholar and teacher, who had come to Rome from Pontus in approximately 68 BCE

ubi, *adv.*, where, when
ulciscor, -ī, ultus sum, to take vengeance, punish
ullus, -a, -um, *adj.*, any
umerus, -ī, *m.*, shoulder
umquam, *adv.*, ever
ūnā, *adv.*, together
undecimus, -a, -um, *adj.*, eleventh
ūniversus, -a, -um, *adj.*, combined in one, whole, entire
ūnus, -a, -um *adj.*, one
urbānitās, -ātis, *f.*, urbanity, politeness, pleasantry; city life
urbānus, -a, -um, *adj.*, of the city, urban, refined, witty, elegant
urbs, urbis, *f.*, city

ūrō, -ere, ussī, ustum, to burn
ūsus, -ūs, *m.,* experience, use
ut, *conj.+ indicative,* as, when; + *subjunctive,* so that, with the result that
utcumque, *adv.,* in whatever manner
uter, utra, utrum, which of the two? the one (of two) which
uterque, utraque, utrumque, each of two, both
ūtilis, -e, *adj.,* useful, valuable
ūtilitās, -ātis, *f.,* usefulness, profit, advantage
utinam, *adv.,* would that! oh that!
ūtor, ūtī, ūsus sum, to use
uxor, -ōris, *f.,* a wife

vacō (1), + *abl.,* to be free from, empty of
valdē, *adv.,* very much, greatly
valeō, -ēre, -uī, -itūrum, to be strong, be well
valētūdo, -inis, *f.,* state of health; good health
validus, -a, -um, *adj.,* powerful, strong, healthy, well
varietās, -ātis, *f.,* variety, difference, diversity
varius, -a, -um, *adj.,* manifold, various
Vatīnius, -ī, *m.,* P. Vatinius, tribune in 59, enemy of Sestius and ally of Julius Caesar; Cicero attacked him bitterly when examining him as a witness during Sestius' trial, but later reconciled with him
vectīgal, -ālis, *n.,* revenue, tax
vector, -ōris, *m.,* carrier, bearer; a passenger
vehementer, *adj.,* violently, vehemently
vehō, -ere, vexī, vectum, to carry, convey
vēlum, -ī, *n.,* sail
vendō, -ere, -didī, -ditum, to sell, put up for sale
venēnum, -ī, *n.,* a drug, poison
veniō, -īre, vēnī, ventum, to come, go
Venusinus, -a, -um, *adj.,* Venusine, referring to the town Venusia, in Apulia on the Appian Way
venustās, -ātis, *f.,* loveliness, beauty, charm, attractiveness
verbum, -ī, *n.,* a word
vereor, -ērī, veritus sum, to fear, respect
vērō, *adv.,* truly, indeed
versō (1), to revolve, turn over; *pass.,* to be about, to be involved in or with, be employed in, take part in
vertō, -ere, versī, versum, to turn
vērum, *adv.,* but, truly
vērus, -a, -um, *adj.,* true, genuine
vester, -tra, -trum, *adj.,* your (pl.)
vestīmentum, -ī, *n.,* clothing, a garment
vetus, -eris, *adj.,* old, former
vetustās, -ātis, *f.,* age, antiquity

vexō (1), to harass, disquiet, annoy; to shake, jostle

via, -ae, *f.*, way, road, street

vibrō (1), to brandish, shake

vicissitūdo, -inis, *f.*, change, alteration

victus, -ūs, *m.*, living, way of living, nourishment, food, support

vīcus, -ī, *m.*, a district of a town or street, an estate, a row of houses

videō, -ēre, vīdī, vīsum, to see

videor, -ērī, vīsus sum, to seem

vigilō (1), to be awake, keep watch

vincō, -ere, vīcī, victum, to conquer, overcome, surpass, win one's point

vir, -ī, *m.*, man

virtūs, -tūtis, *f.*, moral excellence, virtue

vīs, vis, *f.*, force, power, strength

vīta, -ae, *f.*, life

vītalis, -e, *adj.*, vital, of life

vitium, -ī, *n.*, moral fault, vice

vitupero (1), to blame, censure, vituperate

vīvō, -ere, vixī, victum, to live

vix, *adv.*, scarcely, with difficulty, reluctantly

volō, velle, voluī, —, to want, wish, be willing

volūbilitās, -ātis, *f.*, revolving motion; flow of words, fluency

voluptās, -ātis, *f.*, pleasure, delight, enjoyment

vōs, *pron.*, you (pl. of **tu**)

vox, vōcis, *f.*, voice, sound, word

vulgāris *or* **volgāris, -e,** *adj.*, common, ordinary, usual

vultus, -ūs, *m.*, face, expression, look